Diet recommendations for underweight

Please check these recommendations always with a nutrition consultant, therapist, doctor or dietician. The recipes and the list of ingredients are supporting the conventional medical therapy.
The calorie disclosures of fresh ingredients (fruit and vegetables) vary according to quality and time of harvest. The contents were checked by a dietician and a nutrition consultant for the Traditional Chinese Medicine (TCM).

Author:
©2017 Josef Miligui
www.ebns.at

AF285238

Source:
The lists are created from the EBNS database for nutritional counseling. The database is used by dietitians, therapists and doctors for advising the patient / client.

Literature:
The specialist literature and the training documents of the German and Austrian dietary and traditional Chinese medicine serve as a knowledge base. We have used the documents as a basis of knowledge, adapted it to our experience and completed them.
http://di-book.com

Title Photo:
©2008 Erika Weixlbaumer

Production and publishing:
BoD – Books on Demand, Norderstedt
ISBN: 9783752892291

Diet recommendations for DIETETICS - Metabolism - Eating Disorders (Underweight)

1 Treatment strategy

Start with a rich breakfast, as the appetite is usually the strongest in the morning.

Schedule frequent intermediate meals, For example, cream pudding, ice cream, chocolate bar, student food, salt pastry, peanuts.

Try to substitute water for your recipes with whipped cream or milk, so puree, crème soup, dumpling, pancake can be calorie-rich.

Sesame, walnut, sunflower or pumpkin seeds as well as grated cheese in soups, casseroles or salads provide additional calories.

Align soups with egg.

Sweeten compotes and drinks with honey or glucose.

With maltodextrin (pharmacy) they can enrich their drinks, compotes, sauces etc. with calories.

Maltodextrin is a flavor-neutral, boiled and baking starch powder.

If your doctor has prescribed you high-quality food, think of yogurt, plugs and eggs.

Protein concentrates from the pharmacy can be helpful.

Potato-egg combinations such as potato dough, potato swallows with egg, potato butter, alloyed potato soup or also a wheat-milk mixture, Egg dumplings, semolina porridge are useful.

Energy and protein optimization are also provided by industrially produced drinking and supplementary food. These can be drunk in different directions of taste.

2 Avoid

Low calorie foods.

3 Breakfast

4 Snack

5 Lunch

6 Afternoon

7 Dinner

8 Any time

9 Recipes

(recommendable) = You can use more.
(little) = You should use less than specified or omit.

9.1 Andalusian fish pot

Strengthens immune system, prevents cancer, dissolves stagnation, promotes weight loss. Good to fight immunodeficiency, loss of appetite, flatulence, high blood pressure, depressions, diabetes, diarrhea, stimulates appetite.
Cooking time approx. 30 min
Calories p. portion: 348
4 portions
Allergens: ADLO

Quantity of ingredients:
Basic recipe for a vegetable soup (nutritious) 2 cups / 500g. (yes)
Onion (spring onion) 2 pieces / 40g. (yes)
Olive oil 1 table spoon / 20g. (recommended)
Lemon peel 1/2 piece / 3g. (yes)
Bay leaf 1 piece / 1g. (yes)
Potato 5/8 oz / 200g. (yes)
Cod 3/4 lbs / 300g. (yes)
White wine 4 table spoons / 80g. (yes)
Lemon juice 1/2 teaspoon / 10g. (yes)
Salt 1 pinch / 1g. (yes)
Pepper (ground) 1 pinch / 0,2g. (yes)
Parsley 1 table spoon / 15g. (yes)
White bread (wheat bread) 8 slices / 250g. (yes)

Cooking instructions:
Boil the vegetable broth with small spring onion, olive oil, grated lemon peel and bay leaf. Boil covered for 10 minutes. Add the peeled, diced potatoes and boil in about 8 minutes. Add fish pieces and white wine and switch to small heat. In the slightly boiling broth put the fish and boil it a few minutes. Season with lemon juice, salt and pepper. Serve with parsley sprinkled.
White bread as a side dish.

9.2   Avocado with lemon

Good to fight insomnia, inflammation, swelling, pain and itching. Is calming.
Cooking time approx. 5 min
Calories p. portion: 289
1 portions
Allergens:

Quantity of ingredients:
Avocado 1/2 piece / 120g. (recommended)
Lemon juice 1/2 piece / 10g. (yes)
Salt 1 pinch / 1g. (yes)

Cooking instructions:
Halve the avocado, remove the core, add the lemon juice, salt a little and eat with a spoon.

9.3   Barley mash with plums

Promotes spleen, diuretic, forcing spleen, supports urination, relaxes, reduces internal heat.
Cooking time approx. 25 min
Calories p. portion: 107
5 portions
Allergens: AG

Quantity of ingredients:
Water 10 cups / 1200g. (yes)
Barley 1 cup / 120g. (yes)
Plum 1 cup / 120g. (yes)
Butter organic 2 teaspoons / 6g. (recommended)
Sugar cane sugar 1/2 teaspoon / 2g. (recommended)

Cooking instructions:
Grind coarse the barley and roast it dry. Add hot water, add ginger and cardamom and let it swell to a pulp in low heat. Core the plums and boil for 10 minutes with a little water. At the end, add the stewed plums, a little butter and sweetener.

Variant: If you want to go fast, you can use barley flakes instead of shot.

9.4   Basic recipe for a reissue soup (Congee)

Low fat content, for the drainage of the body overweight and high blood pressure.
Cooking time approx. 2-4 hours
Calories p. portion: 140
3 portions
Allergens:

Quantity of ingredients:
Rice variety any 1 cup / 120g. (yes)
Water 6 cups / 700g. (yes)

Cooking instructions:
Cook rice and water in a ratio of about 1: 6. The amount of water determines the thickness of the mash (matter of taste).
Put the rice in a saucepan with a heavy lid. It is important to simmer the rice after a short boil on the slightest flame, otherwise it burns.
Boil the rice for 2-4 hours. The longer he cooks, the more he strengthens.
If you want to eat the dish for breakfast, you can put the rice on just before bedtime.
To be on the safe side, you should first check the behavior of your pot and cooker under observation for a similar amount of time, so that nothing burns.
Refrigerate for later use.

9.5   Basic recipe for a vegetable soup, nutritious

Reduces blood pressure, strengthens immune system, prevents cancer, forcing spleen, dissolves stagnation, promotes weight loss. Good to fight immunodeficiency, high blood pressure, depressions, diabetes, diarrhea, reduces blood lipids.
Cooking time approx. 2-3 hours
Calories p. portion: 48
5 portions
Allergens: L

Quantity of ingredients:
Olive oil 1 table spoon / 4g. (recommended)
Onion white 1 piece / 60g. (yes)
Carrot 3 pieces / 200g. (yes)

Parsnip 3/8 lbs - 6oz / 150g. (yes)
Celery root 1 cup / 100g. (yes)
Ginger fresh 1/2 teaspoon / 2g. (yes)
Lemon 1/2 piece / 25g. (yes)
Juniper berry 6 pieces / 6g. (yes)
Thyme dried 1 pinch / 1g. (yes)
Lovage 1 table spoon / 3g. (yes)
Bay leaf 2 leaves / 1g. (yes)
Salt 1 pinch / 1g. (yes)
Water 3 cups / 650g. (yes)

Cooking instructions:
Cut the vegetables into cubes.
Heat oil in hot pot, fry shortly onions and vegetables.
Add cold water, then add ginger, bay leaf and lemon juice.
Season with juniper, thyme and lovage. Cover for 2 - 3 hours on a low heat and simmer.
The used vegetables should be thrown away.
The basic recipe serves as a soup base and to refine vegetables, legumes or cereals.
If you want to eat vegetable soup immediately, add the desired vegetables half an hour before.
Refrigerate for later use.

9.6 Beef broth

Warming and nourishing, forces.
Cooking time approx. 2-6 hours
Calories p. portion: 125
7 portions
Allergens: L

Quantity of ingredients:
Water 4 cup / 1000g. (yes)
Lemon 2 daches / 2g. (yes)
Beef meat 1,1 lbs / 500g. (yes)
Beef meatbones 2 pieces / 0g. (yes)
Turmeric (yellow root) 1 pinch / 1g. (yes)
Carrot 2 pieces / 100g. (yes)
Celery root 1 inch / 25g. (yes)
Parsley root 1 piece / 150g. (yes)

Onion white 1 piece / 50g. (yes)
Bay leaf 2-3 leaves / 2g. (yes)
Coriander 1/2 teaspoon / 2g. (yes)
Ginger fresh 1 inch / 2g. (yes)
Wakame 1 inch / 1g. (yes)
Parsley 1 stem / 10g. (yes)

Cooking instructions:
In a saucepan with water (enough to cover the meat), add a few drops
of lemon juice, a little turmeric, beef and bones, heat till it boils and
simmer for a while; then pour away the whole broth, clean the pot, rinse
off meat and bones with hot water (this will save you from foaming) and
put it back to the saucepan with hot water (amount as you like); add a
good pinch of turmeric, carrot, celery, parsley root to the pot; add onion,
bay leaves, coriander, a piece of sliced ginger, a strip of wakame, a
stalk of parsley; boil everything together and simmer for 2-6 hours (if the
meat is to be used otherwise, take it out of the broth after 1 1/2 - 2
hours, as soon as it is cooked, the bones are returned to the broth);
When the cooking time is over, pour the broth through a sieve and
discard all ingredients.

Notes: The longer the broth has cooked, the warmer but more
nourishing it is. It is after cooling for 3-4 days in the refrigerator durable.
The broth can be drunk hot or used as a base for soups with cereals,
potatoes and fresh vegetables.

9.7 Beef pumpkin and vegetable stew

Reduces inflammation, improves digestion, reduces blood glucose,
strengthens the muscles, tendons and bones, promotes digestion, helps
to digest fat.
Cooking time approx. 1 hour
Calories p. portion: 369
4 portions
Allergens: AL

Quantity of ingredients:
Beef meat 3/4 lbs / 350g. (yes)
Pumpkin 3/4 lbs / 350g. (yes)
Leek 3/8 lbs - 6oz / 150g. (yes)
Potato 3/4 lbs / 350g. (yes)
Tomato 3/8 lbs - 6oz / 150g. (yes)
Olive oil 2 table spoons / 25g. (recommended)

Basic recipe for a vegetable soup 1/4 lbs - 4oz / 125g. (yes)
Salt 1 pinch / 1g. (yes)
Pepper (ground) 1 pinch / 0,5g. (yes)
Peppers powder 1 teaspoon / 2g. (yes)
Ground caraway 1 pinch / 1g. (yes)
Sugar cane sugar 1 pinch / 1g. (recommended)
Parsley 1/2 bunch / 30g. (yes)
White bread (wheat bread) 4 slices / 80g. (yes)

Cooking instructions:
Dice beef. Peel pumpkin and dice. Cut the leek into rings and dice the peeled potatoes.
Brew the tomatoes with boiling water, peel off the skin and dice.
Steam the meat in olive oil and fill with vegetable stock. Add the cleaned vegetables. Season with salt, pepper, paprika, cumin and fructose.
Stew for 30 minutes over low heat.
Season again and sprinkle with parsley and serve with white bread.

9.8   Bircher-muesli with yogurt, nuts and apple

Fibre-rich, relieves constipation, strengthens immune system, forcing spleen, promotes weight loss. Good to fight immunodeficiency, loss of appetite.
Cooking time approx. 2 hours and more
Calories p. portion: 383
1 portions
Allergens: AGH

Quantity of ingredients:
Muesli 2 table spoons / 20g. (yes)
Oat flakes (whole grain) 2 table spoons / 20g. (yes)
Yogurt (natural, 3.5% fat) 6 table spoons / 80g. (recommended)
Lemon 1 table spoon / 10g. (yes)
Acerola fruit nectar or powder 1/2 teaspoon / 1g. (yes)
Apple (sour) 1 piece / 170g. (yes)
Hazelnuts 1 table spoon / 10g. (recommended)

Cooking instructions:
Soak oatmeal in the yogurt for several hours in the fridge. Add rubed nuts, lemon juice, acerola, grated apple. For sweets, raisins can be used.

9.9   Carrot and millet bake with apple compote

Promotes spleen and liver, reduces blood pressure, strengthens immune system, prevents cancer, reduces radiation damage, calms nerves and stomach, good to fight chronic constipation of the intestine.
Cooking time approx. 1 hour
Calories p. portion: 350
7 portions
Allergens: CGH

Quantity of ingredients:
Millet 5/8 oz / 200g. (yes)
Cow's milk (whole milk 3.5% fat) 2 cups / 450g. (recommended)
Lemon peel 1/2 piece / 2g. (yes)
Sugar brown 2 table spoons / 20g. (recommended)
Carrot 7/8 lbs / 400g. (yes)
Ginger fresh 2 teaspoons / 6g. (yes)
Acerola fruit nectar or powder 1 teaspoon / 2g. (yes)
Almond puree 1/8 lbs - 2oz / 50g. (yes)
Chicken egg 4 pieces / 240g. (yes)
Yogurt (natural, 1.5% fat) 3/8 lbs - 6oz / 150g. (yes)
Butter organic 1 teaspoon / 4g. (recommended)
Apple (sour) 4 pieces / 600g. (yes)
Water 1 cup / 300g. (yes)
Clove 2 pieces / 1g. (yes)
Sugar brown 1 table spoon / 10g. (recommended)

Cooking instructions:
Preheat the oven to 100°C/212°F (with circulating air 8o°C/176°F, gas level 2).
Heat the milk with the millet till it boils, add lemon zest and sugar. Cover and simmer for 5 minutes, then simmer in a preheated oven for 20 minutes. Switch oven to medium heat.
Peel apples and cut into small pieces, boil with water, cloves and sugar for about 5 minutes.
Mix the millet in a bowl with the grated carrots, finely chopped ginger and acerola.
Mix the almond paste (or butter) with the hand mixer. Add egg yolk and stir everything to a smooth cream. Mix in sour cream. Add millet and carrots.
Beat the egg whites very stiff and lift them under the millet pulp. Brush out a baking dish with butter. Add the millet and bake in a preheated oven for 45 minutes on a low heat. Serve with the apple compote.

9.10 Cottage cheese with steamed fruit

Good to fight loss of appetite, promotes digestion, supports urination.
Cooking time approx. 20 min
Calories p. portion: 214
2 portions
Allergens: G

Quantity of ingredients:
Cottage cheese 3/4 lbs / 300g. (yes)
Apple (sour) 1 piece / 100g. (yes)
Pear 1 piece / 100g. (yes)

Cooking instructions:
Wash apples and pears well, do not peel, and chop small. In a pot with steam filter, boil them al dente, remove and allow to cool down.
Serve the cheese, spread the fruit on it.

9.11 Cranberry juice

Antibacterial, good to fight loss of appetite, arteriosclerosis, bladder infections, diarrhea, colds. Antipyretic, against free radicals, gout, diuretic, stomach ulcers, oral mucosa inflammation, rheumatism.
Cooking time approx. 5 min
Calories p. portion: 43
1 portions
Allergens:

Quantity of ingredients:
Cranberries 2 table spoons / 25g. (yes)
Water 1 cup / 125g. (yes)
Honey 1 table spoon / 10g. (yes)

Cooking instructions:
Mix the cranberries with a little water with the blender to a pulp. Add the remaining water and sweeten with the honey.

9.12 Curdcheesedumplings on strawberry pulp

Strawberry forcing spleen and stomach, strengthens blood. Chicken egg calms nerves and stomach.
Cooking time approx. 30 min
Calories p. portion: 553
5 portions

Allergens: ACG

Quantity of ingredients:
Curd cheese 20% 1,1 lbs / 500g. (yes)
Spelled semolina 3/8 lbs - 6oz / 150g. (yes)
Butter organic 1/8 lbs - 2oz / 40g. (recommended)
Chicken egg 2 pieces / 120g. (yes)
Sugar - icing sugar 2 table spoons / 20g. (recommended)
Salt 1 pinch / 1g. (yes)
Breadcrumbs (wheat bread, bread roll) 2 table spoons / 25g. (yes)
Butter organic 1/4 lbs - 4oz / 100g. (recommended)
Strawberries 1,1 lbs / 500g. (yes)
Sugar - icing sugar 2 table spoons / 25g. (recommended)

Cooking instructions:
Curdcheese, grit, butter, eggs, powdered sugar and salt to a smooth dough. Keep the dough 15 mins in the refrigerator to settle down. Then shape small dumplings with a diameter of approx 4cm and boil them for about 10 minutes in slightly boiling salt water. Heat butter in a pan and roast the breadcrumbs golden brown. Roll the dumplings carefully into the crumbs.
Serve the dumplings with the strawberry.

9.13 Duck with mung beans

Strengthens blood, forcing spleen, supports urination, promotes spleen and liver, reduces blood pressure, strengthens immune system, prevents cancer, reduces radiation damage, dissolves stagnation.
Cooking time approx. 2 hours
Calories p. portion: 747
5 portions
Allergens: E

Quantity of ingredients:
Duck (slaughtered) 1/2 piece / 1250g. (recommended)
Onion white 2 pieces / 120g. (yes)
Carrot 1 piece / 120g. (yes)
Garlic 1 clove / 3g. (yes)
Mung bean 5/8 lbs - 8oz / 250g. (yes)
Peppercorns 3 pieces / 2g. (yes)
Honey 1 teaspoon / 3g. (yes)
Soy sauce 1 teaspoon / 3g. (yes)
Lemon juice 1 teaspoon / 3g. (yes)

Salt 1 pinch / 1g. (yes)
Pepper (ground) 1 pinch / 0,5g. (yes)
Olive oil 1 table spoon / 10g. (recommended)
Bay leaf 2 leaves / 2g. (yes)
Black caraway 1 pinch / 1g. (yes)
Savory 1 teaspoon / 2g. (yes)

Cooking instructions:
The day before soak the mung beans and rinse the duck cold. Wash
the vegetables, clean and cut into pieces. Put the duck and vegetables
in a saucepan and cover with water. Add bay leaves, savory, mugwort
and peppercorns. Boil over medium heat and simmer for 45 minutes.
Skim off the foam. Remove duck from the stock, allow to cool and keep
cool overnight.

In a saucepan, sauté the chopped onion in olive oil and pour in 1/4 liter
of stock and add the pre-cooked vegetables. Add the mung beans and
season with honey, soy sauce, lemon juice, salt, crushed black cumin
and pepper.

Serve with rice or potatoes.

9.14 Exotic lenses

Strengthens heart and kidney, diuretic, calms the stomach, promotes
digestion, dissolves stagnation, helps to digest fat, supports urination,
reduces blood pressure, detoxifying and stimulating the immune
system.
Cooking time approx. 45 min
Calories p. portion: 144
4 portions
Allergens: NO

Quantity of ingredients:
Sesame oil 1 table spoon / 10g. (recommended)
Onion white 2 pieces / 120g. (yes)
Ginger fresh 1/2 teaspoon / 2g. (yes)
Thyme dried 1/2 teaspoon / 1g. (yes)
Cumin (Caraway seed) 1/2 teaspoon / 2g. (yes)
Lentils red 1 cup / 120g. (yes)
Wakame 1 inch / 1g. (yes)

Lemon 1/2 piece / 20g. (yes)
Bocksdorn fruits (Fructus Lycii, 2 pinches / 2g. (yes)
Sugar cane sugar 1 pinch / 1g. (recommended)
Salt 1 pinch / 1g. (yes)
Vinegar (Apple vinegar) 1/2 teaspoon / 1g. (yes)
Tomato 1 piece / 50g. (yes)
Chard 5/8 oz / 200g. (yes)
Cauliflower 5/8 oz / 200g. (yes)
Salt 1 pinch / 1g. (yes)
Rice (whole grain) 1/2 cup / 60g. (yes)
Water 3 cups / 300g. (yes)
Salt 1 pinch / 1g. (yes)

Cooking instructions:
Heat sesame oil in a hot pot. Add chopped onions, grated ginger, dried thyme, plenty of cumin and sauté gently.
Add peeled red lentils, a strip of wakame, a little lemon juice, hot water and some dried buckthorn fruits. Simmer for 20 minutes until the lentils are cooked; add hot water as needed to make a pulp. Add sugar, some chili and salt.
Add vinegar or lemon juice depending on your taste. Add chopped tomatoes as desired. Let it pass for a few minutes.

Cook in a small pot with 1 cup of water and a little salt the cauliflower 10 min. until soft.

Blanch in a small pot with 1 cup of water and salt the chard 3 min.

Boil the rice briefly, salt and 10 min. to let go. Serve everything with the lentil dish.

9.15 Fast polenta with avocado and spring onion

Good to fight inflammations, swelling, pain. Forcing spleen and stomach, lets urine and bile juice flow, dissolves stagnation. Includes unsaturated fatty acids, antioxidativ.
Cooking time approx. 10 min
Calories p. portion: 450
2 portions
Allergens:

Quantity of ingredients:
Corn (fast polenta) 1 cup / 120g. (yes)
Water 1 1/2 cups / 240g. (yes)
Olive oil 1 table spoon / 15g. (recommended)
Salt 1 pinch / 1g. (yes)
Pepper (ground) 1 pinch / 0,5g. (yes)
Lemon juice 1 dash / 3g. (yes)
Onion (spring onion) 2 pieces / 40g. (yes)
Avocado 1/2 piece / 150g. (recommended)
Turmeric (yellow root) 1 pinch / 1g. (yes)
Basil (fresh) 1 teaspoon / 2g. (yes)

Cooking instructions:
Heat water, add oil, lemon and spices.
When the water boils, add the polenta while stirring constantly and cook for 2 minutes.
When the porridge becomes firm, the polenta is ready.
Add diced avocado and sliced spring onion to the polenta. Sprinkle fresh basil on it.

9.16 Fennel with roasted walnuts

Forcing spleen, detoxifying, reduces inflammation, improves blood circulation, improves medication effect, stimulates appetite, antioxidativ, promotes digestion, stimulates, dissolves stagnation.
Cooking time approx. 20 min
Calories p. portion: 342
4 portions
Allergens: HO

Quantity of ingredients:
Fennel 4 pieces / 800g. (yes)
Nutmeg 1 pinch / 1g. (yes)
Ginger fresh 1/2 teaspoon / 1g. (yes)
Salt 1 pinch / 1g. (yes)
White wine 1/2 cup / 125g. (yes)
Peppers powder 1 pinch / 1g. (yes)
Olive oil 2 table spoons / 40g. (recommended)
Walnuts 2 table spoons / 35g. (recommended)
Water 1 1/2 cups / 220g. (yes)
Corn Grease (Polenta) 1 cup / 120g. (yes)
Salt 1 pinch / 1g. (yes)

Cooking instructions:
Heat very little water in a pot; Fry the fennel in strips. Add Nutmeg, a little grated ginger, add salt, a dash of white wine, rose paprika.
Simmer until the vegetables are cooked, but still crisp; stir in a little olive oil; sprinkle with roasted walnuts.

Stir the polenta into a pot of hot water, stirring constantly, until the polenta has the desired consistency. Salt.
Pull the polenta off the fire and let it swell for about 10 minutes.

9.17 Fried apple

Good to fight acute or chronic constipation of the intestine, warming stomach and spleen, improves blood circulation. Good to fight kidney weakness, back pain and abdominal pain, impotence.
Cooking time approx. 30 min
Calories p. portion: 408
4 portions
Allergens: GH

Quantity of ingredients:
Apple (sour) 4 pieces / 500g. (yes)
Hazelnuts 1/8 lbs - 2oz / 50g. (recommended)
Almond 1/8 lbs - 2oz / 50g. (recommended)
Cinnamon ground 1 pinch / 0,2g. (yes)
Vanilla sugar natural 1 package / 3g. (yes)
Cow's milk (whole milk 3.5% fat) 2 table spoons / 24g. (recommended)
Sugar - icing sugar 2 table spoons / 36g. (recommended)
Cinnamon ground 1 pinch / 1g. (yes)
Yoghurt vanilla 3 cups / 750g. (yes)

Cooking instructions:
Wash the apples, cut off a lid, cut out the core casing with a teaspoon so that the apple remains a tight bottom.
Mix nuts, almonds, fructose, milk, vanilla sugar, cinnamon well. Fill into the apples. Put the covers back on.
Bake in preheated oven at 180 ° C for approx. 20 minutes.
Mix icing sugar and cinnamon.
Spread vanilla yoghurt on plate, place 1 baked apple on each, sprinkle with cinnamon-powdered sugar mixture.
Serve hot immediately!

9.18 Grilled tomatoes with cheese filling

Promotes digestion, helps to digest fat, supports urination, reduces blood pressure, stimulates digestion.
Cooking time approx. 30 min
Calories p. portion: 470
2 portions
Allergens: ACG

Quantity of ingredients:
Tomato 8 pieces / 200g. (yes)
Feta cheese 0,2 lbs / 75g. (yes)
Fresh cheese 0,2 lbs / 75g. (yes)
Chicken egg 1 piece / 60g. (yes)
Olive oil 1 table spoon / 12g. (recommended)
Basil (fresh) 1 table spoon / 6g. (yes)
Salt 1 pinch / 1g. (yes)
Pepper (ground) 1 pinch / 0,5g. (yes)
Olives 1 oz / 30g. (recommended)
Rucola 1/4 lbs / 100g. (yes)
White bread (wheat bread) 4 slices / 80g. (yes)

Cooking instructions:
Hollow out tomatoes generously. Put in a casserole dish.
Mix cheese, olive oil, egg, chopped basil and flour. Season with salt and pepper and fill in the tomatoes.
Bake in the preheated oven at 210 degrees on the middle rail for 15 minutes, then switch on the oven grill and grill for a further 3 minutes (without circulating air).
Stone the olives and chop and sprinkle on the tomatoes.
Garnish tomatoes with rocket and serve with white bread.

9.19 Halibut with tomato and garlic sauce

Promotes digestion, helps to digest fat, supports urination, reduces blood pressure, good to fight rheumatism, flatulence, bladder weakness, anemia, high blood pressure, depressions, diabetes, diarrhea. Valuable omega-3 fatty acids.
Cooking time approx. 45 min
Calories p. portion: 319
5 portions
Allergens: D

Quantity of ingredients:
Rice variety any 1 cup / 120g. (yes)
Water 6 cups / 240g. (yes)
Salt 1 pinch / 1g. (yes)
Halibut (Flatfish) 2,2 lbs / 800g. (yes)
Salt 1 pinch / 1g. (yes)
Pepper (ground) 1 pinch / 0,5g. (yes)
Lemon juice 1 dach / 2g. (yes)
Bay leaf 2 pieces / 2g. (yes)
Lemon 1 piece / 30g. (yes)
Garlic 8 pieces / 10g. (yes)
Thyme dried 1 table spoon / 5g. (yes)
Olives 0,2 lbs / 75g. (recommended)
Tomato 4 pieces / 200g. (yes)
Salt 1 pinch / 1g. (yes)
Pepper (ground) 1 pinch / 0,5g. (yes)

Cooking instructions:
Cook rice with salted water (1:3).
Rinse the fish under running cold water, dab with kitchen paper and rub with salt, pepper and lemon juice.
Place the fish fillets in a casserole dish with pieces of bay leaf.

Wash the lemon hot and cut into slices, peel and halve the garlic.
Sprinkle the olives and the thyme over them.
Brew the tomatoes with hot water, skin and chop.

Mix all ingredients, season with salt and pepper and distribute around the fish.

Cook everything at 200°C/392°F for about 20 minutes.
Serve with the rice.

9.20 Hearty polenta mash

Strengths spleen and stomach, promotes watering, promotes digestion, detoxifying, promotes perspiration, reduces blood lipids, stimulates, dissolves stagnation, stimulates appetite, dissolves stagnation.
Cooking time approx. 10 min
Calories p. portion: 262
2 portions
Allergens:

Quantity of ingredients:
Corn Grease (Polenta) 1 cup / 120g. (yes)
Onion (spring onion) 2 pieces / 40g. (yes)
Ginger fresh 1/2 teaspoon / 2g. (yes)
Nutmeg 1 pinch / 1g. (yes)
Salt 1 pinch / 1g. (yes)
Olive oil 1 table spoon / 10g. (recommended)
Turmeric (yellow root) 1 pinch / 1g. (yes)
Water 1 1/2 cups / 240g. (yes)

Cooking instructions:
Stir in the polenta in boiling water and let it swell for 7 min. Add green onion, grated ginger, turmeric, nutmeg, salt and olive oil and wait for 3 more minutes.

9.21 Lettuce with fresh cheese

The bitter substances have diuretic effect and promote the blood circulation in the digestive area. Mustard improves thyroid function, relieves rheumatism symptoms.
Cooking time approx. 5 min
Calories p. portion: 802
1 portions
Allergens: AFM

Quantity of ingredients:
Leaf salads (bitter) 2 portions / 60g. (yes)
Fresh cheese from soya 3/8 lbs - 6oz / 150g. (yes)
Mustard 1 knife tip / 1g. (yes)
Lemon juice 1 dash / 3g. (yes)
Salt 1 pinch / 1g. (yes)
Pepper (ground) 1 pinch / 0,5g. (yes)
Herbs various 2 teaspoons / 4g. (yes)
Black caraway 1 pinch / 1g. (yes)
Whole grain bread 2 slices / 40g. (yes)

Cooking instructions:
Wash lettuce and finely pluck.
Mix 150 ml cream cheese, splashes of mustard, splashes of lemon juice, 1 clove of garlic, chopped fresh herbs, pinch of pepper and crushed black cumin and pour over. Serve with wholemeal bread.

9.22 Marinated cod on pumpkin puree

Reduces inflammation, improves digestion, promotes spleen, lung, stomach and kidneys, diuretic, reduces blood glucose, good to fight constipation and flatulence, dissolves stagnation.
Cooking time approx. 2 hours
Calories p. portion: 202
4 portions
Allergens: DG

Quantity of ingredients:
Potato 6 pieces / 400g. (yes)
Pumpkin 5/8 oz / 200g. (yes)
Onion white 1 piece / 50g. (yes)
Oregano dried 1/2 teaspoon / 1g. (yes)
Lemon juice 1/2 piece / 15g. (yes)
Salt 1 pinch / 1g. (yes)
Pepper (ground) 1 pinch / 0,3g. (yes)
Créme fraiche cheese 2 table spoons / 30g. (recommended)
Yogurt (natural, 1.5% fat) 3/8 lbs - 6oz / 150g. (yes)
Oregano dried 1/4 teaspoon / 1g. (yes)
Basil (fresh) 1/2 teaspoon / 2g. (yes)
Cod 3/4 lbs / 300g. (yes)
Salt 1 pinch / 1g. (yes)
Pepper (ground) 1 pinch / 0,3g. (yes)
Olive oil 1 teaspoon / 3g. (recommended)

Cooking instructions:
Mix yoghurt with oregano, basil and thyme.
Wash the fish fillets, pat dry, place in a flat shape and pour over the marinade. Leave 2 hours in refrigerator.

Cook the potatoes in salted water until soft and peel.

Sauté the onion in oil until glassy, add the diced pumpkin and cook for about 10 min. Add oregano, lemon juice, salt, pepper and crème fraiche and puree with the blender.

Remove fish fillets from the marinade, drain, pat dry and salt. Coat a coated grill pan with 2 teaspoons of oil. Roast the fish fillets on both sides for 3 - 4 minutes and arrange with the potatoes on the pumpkin puree.

9.23 Melanzani with olive oil and turmeric

improves blood circulation, reduces inflammation, relieves pain, promotes digestion, helps to digest fat, supports urination, reduces blood pressure.
Cooking time approx. 30 min
Calories p. portion: 432
2 portions
Allergens: A

Quantity of ingredients:
Aubergine 2 pieces / 300g. (yes)
Olive oil 4 table spoons / 60g. (recommended)
Tomato 4 pieces / 200g. (yes)
Turmeric (yellow root) 1/2 teaspoon / 1g. (yes)
Ground 1 pinch / 1g. (yes)
Salt 1 pinch / 1g. (yes)
White bread (wheat bread) 4 slices / 80g. (yes)

Cooking instructions:
Cut the melanzani into slices and spread them with the tomatoes on a baking tray. Sprinkle with olive oil and then with turmeric, caraway and salt. Bake them in the tube 20 min.
Serve with the white bread.

9.24 Millet with pears

Refreshing and nourishing, promotes digestion, supports urination, good to fight cough, promotes perspiration, reduces blood lipids, stimulates, dissolves stagnation, forces liver, strengthens the muscles, lowers cholesterol, antiparasitic.
Cooking time approx. 35 min
Calories p. portion: 213
5 portions
Allergens: G

Quantity of ingredients:
Millet 1 cup / 120g. (yes)
Water 1 1/2 cups / 200g. (yes)
Grape juice red 1 1/2 cups / 240g. (yes)
Pear 4 pieces / 600g. (yes)
Ginger fresh 1/2 teaspoon / 2g. (yes)
Salt 1 pinch / 1g. (yes)
Acerola fruit nectar or powder 1 teaspoon / 2g. (yes)

Cocoa 1 pinch / 1g. (yes)
Sunflower seeds 2 table spoons / 4g. (recommended)
Barley malt 1/2 teaspoon / 2g. (yes)
Cream, sweet 30% 2 teaspoons / 20g. (recommended)

Cooking instructions:
Simmer the millet for 5 min and let it swell for another 30 min.

Then: In a hot pot, heat some grape juice; add chopped pears, very little grated ginger, a pinch of salt, acerola, a pinch of cocoa and sauté briefly; add the boiled millet, sunflower seeds, some barley malt to taste, 1 tsp cream per serving or a little butter.

9.25 Noodle casserole with plugs and peaches

Relieves fatigue, relaxes, good to fight belching, acute or chronic obstruction of the bowel, flatulence, heartburn. Calms nerves and stomach, strengthens the defense, good to fight fungi infections.
Cooking time approx. 1 hour
Calories p. portion: 442
4 portions
Allergens: ACGO

Quantity of ingredients:
Peaches 1,1 lbs / 500g. (yes)
Noodles (wheat, ribbon noodles) with egg 5/8 oz / 200g. (yes)
Chicken egg 2 pieces / 120g. (yes)
Sugar - icing sugar 1/8 lbs - 2oz / 40g. (recommended)
Vanilla sugar natural 3 package / 3g. (yes)
Lemon peel 1/2 piece / 2g. (yes)
Cinnamon ground 1/4 teaspoon / 1g. (yes)
Curd cheese 20% 5/8 lbs - 8oz / 250g. (yes)
Butter organic 2 teaspoons / 8g. (recommended)
Strawberry jam 4 table spoons / 50g. (yes)

Cooking instructions:
Preheat oven to 180°C/356°F.
Put Peaches briefly in boiling water, drain and peel off the skin. Cut peaches into small slices.
Cook noodles in plenty of salted water until firm, drain, chill off cold and drain.
Separate eggs. Stir egg yolks with icing sugar, vanilla sugar, grated lemon zest and cinnamon until fluffy with the whisk. Stir in the curd

cheese. Add the noodles.

Beat the egg whites into firm snow and carefully lift them under the pasta.

Spread a baking dish thinly with butter. Alternating pate noodle mixture and peach slices into the form layers. Finish with the pasta mixture. Sprinkle the casserole with butter flakes and bake in a preheated oven for 3o minutes.

Serve portion by portion with a tablespoon of jam.

9.26 Noodles with turkeymeat and pineapple

Solves bile-, kidney- and bladder stones, provides Vitamin C, strengthens blood, strengthens bone marrow, reduces inflammation, supports urination.
Cooking time approx. 45 min
Calories p. portion: 292
4 portions
Allergens: ACGL

Quantity of ingredients:
Noodles (whole grain) with egg 5/8 oz / 200g. (yes)
Pineapple 5/8 oz / 200g. (yes)
Water 1/2 cup / 50g. (yes)
Turkey breast meat 5/8 oz / 200g. (yes)
Rapeseed oil 1 table spoon / 12g. (recommended)
Garlic 1 piece / 2g. (yes)
Basic recipe for a vegetable soup (nutritious) 1/2 cup / 100g. (yes)
Cow's milk (whole milk 3.5% fat) 2/3 cup / 180g. (recommended)
Fresh cheese 0,2 lbs / 75g. (yes)
Curry 3 teaspoons / 6g. (yes)
Salt 1 pinch / 1g. (yes)
Pepper (ground) 1 pinch / 0,5g. (yes)
Pomegranate 1 piece / 300g. (yes)
Coconut flakes 1 table spoon / 6g. (yes)

Cooking instructions:
Cook the noodles in salt water. Cut the pineapple into cubes and leave for 5 min. to simmer in water. Cut the meat sliced in strips and roast them in the oil. Add the chopped garlic and the pineapple sliced. Add about 50 ml of the ananas juice and stir in the vegetable broth. Add the milk and the fresh cheese, then stir well until the fresh cheese is completely dissolved. Now add the curry and simmer for a few minutes until a creamy consistency is reached.

Season with salt and pepper. Now add the noodles in the finished sauce. Cut the pomegranate and release the seeds. Distribute as many kernels on the dressed noodles. Whoever likes it can spread coconut chips over it.

9.27 Noodles with vegetable and tomato sauce

Protects the digestive system. Detoxifying, Good to fight loss of appetite, flatulence, inflammatory bowel disease, obesity, gout, stomach ulcers, stomach cramps, rheumatism, heartburn, twelffinger intestinal ulcers, promotes digestion, helps to digest fat.
Cooking time approx. 45 min
Calories p. portion: 562
2 portions
Allergens: ACG

Quantity of ingredients:
Tomato 1/4 lbs - 4oz / 125g. (yes)
Carrot 1 piece / 80g. (yes)
Zucchini 1 piece / 80g. (yes)
Olive oil 1 table spoon / 15g. (recommended)
Onion (shallot) 1 piece / 20g. (yes)
Oregano dried 1 pinch / 1g. (yes)
Salt 1 pinch / 1g. (yes)
Pepper (ground) 1 pinch / 0,2g. (yes)
Noodles (wheat) with egg 5/8 oz / 200g. (yes)
Olive oil 1 table spoon / 10g. (recommended)
Créme fraiche cheese 2 table spoons / 30g. (recommended)

Cooking instructions:
Boil the tomatoes with a little water, drain and collect the juice, cut the tomatoes into pieces.
Roughly grate zucchini and carrot. Heat olive oil in a pot. Steam shallots very soft. Add tomatoes, season with oregano, salt and pepper. Simmer tomatoes to a thick sauce.
Bring plenty of salted water to boil, cook the wholegrain noodles until firm.
In the cooking time of the pasta, heat in a pan olive oil. Fry the carrots while stirring, lightly salt. Add zucchini, sauté briefly while stirring. The vegetables should be soft with a bite.
Drain pasta, mix with créme fraiche, season with salt and pepper.
Garnish with the tomato sauce.

9.28 Oat flakes with aromatic spices

Stops diarrhea, promotes digestion, appetizing, harmonizes the stomach, detoxifying and stimulating the immune system.
Cooking time approx. 25 min
Calories p. portion: 280
3 portions
Allergens: AH

Quantity of ingredients:
Oat flakes (whole grain) 1 cup / 125g. (yes)
Walnuts 1 table spoon / 15g. (recommended)
Hazelnuts 1 table spoon / 15g. (recommended)
Water 1 1/2 cups / 240g. (yes)
Wakame 1 inch / 2g. (yes)
Apple (sweet) 1 piece / 220g. (yes)
Cardamom 3-4 capsules / 2g. (yes)
Lemon Balm (fresh) 3-4 leaves / 3g. (yes)
Acerola fruit nectar or powder 1 teaspoon / 2g. (yes)

Cooking instructions:
Roast oatmeal and nuts. Add hot water. Add cardamom, wakame and cook for 20 min. Add grated apple, acerola and lemon herb.

9.29 Oriental rice pan

Forcing spleen, promotes weight loss. Good to fight immunodeficiency, loss of appetite, flatulence, high blood pressure, helps to digest fat.
Numerous vitamins, minerals and secondary plant active ingredients.
Cooking time approx. 30 min
Calories p. portion: 303
6 portions
Allergens: EL

Quantity of ingredients:
Rice (whole grain) 3/8 lbs - 6oz / 180g. (yes)
Basic recipe for a vegetable soup (nutritious) 2 1/4 cups / 500g. (yes)
Curry 1/2 teaspoon / 2g. (yes)
Onion (spring onion) 4 pieces / 80g. (yes)
Rapeseed oil 2 table spoons / 20g. (recommended)
Peppers 1/4 lbs - 4oz / 120g. (yes)
Corn 3 oz / 80g. (yes)
Shiitake, dried 1/2 oz / 80g. (yes)
Bamboo shoots 3 oz / 80g. (yes)

Peas 3 oz / 80g. (yes)
Peaches 1/8 lbs - 2oz / 60g. (yes)
Pineapple 1/8 lbs - 2oz / 60g. (yes)
Tomato 5/8 oz / 200g. (yes)
Lovage 1 teaspoon / 2g. (yes)
Basil (fresh) 1 teaspoon / 2g. (yes)
Parsley 1 teaspoon / 2g. (yes)
Lemon Balm (fresh) 1 teaspoon / 2g. (yes)
Pepper (ground) 1 pinch / 1g. (yes)

Cooking instructions:
Soak the mushrooms in water 20 min.
Boil the rice in the vegetable stock 15 min. and season with some curry.
Peel the onion, cut into fine cubes.
Heat the oil in a pan and sauté the onion cubes.
Wash the peppers in half, remove the core, cut into cubes and add.
Add corn, mushrooms and bamboo shoots, simmer 5 min. until firm.
Also add the bean sprouts, peas, peach cubes and pineapple cubes.
Then add the peeled, chopped tomatoes.
Add the cooked rice and season with the herbs and pepper.

9.30 Oven potatoes with celery-curd cheese (quark)

Promotes spleen, reduces Inflammation, improves digestion,
regenerates skin, supports urination, lowers cholesterol.
Cooking time approx. 30 min
Calories p. portion: 304
2 portions
Allergens: GL

Quantity of ingredients:
Celery root 3 oz / 80g. (yes)
Basic recipe for a vegetable soup (nutritious) 1/2 cup / 100g. (yes)
Ground caraway 1 pinch / 0,2g. (yes)
Lemon peel 1/2 teaspoon / 1g. (yes)
Salt 1 pinch / 1g. (yes)
Pepper (ground) 1 pinch / 0,2g. (yes)
Lemon juice 1 teaspoon / 3g. (yes)
Curd cheese 20% 5/8 oz / 200g. (yes)
Créme fraiche cheese 1/2 teaspoon / 5g. (recommended)
Potato 6 pieces / 400g. (yes)
Olive oil 2 teaspoons / 5g. (recommended)
Salt 1 pinch / 1g. (yes)

Cooking instructions:
Celery-curd cheese:
Mix celery with vegetable broth according to basic recipe, caraway and lemon peel. Cook for about 8 minutes until the celery is soft and the vegetable broth almost evaporated. Mix the celery vegetable broth with the lemon juice, finely, and stir until smooth. Season with salt and pepper.

Baked potatoes:
Preheat oven to 200 °C / 400 °F.
Brush the potatoes well, halve them, and place them on a baking tray with the cut surface facing up. Lightly salt the surfaces and sprinkle with oil. Fry the potatoes in the oven for about 25 minutes.
Serve the celery plug to the potatoes.

9.31 Pancakes with spinach and parmesan

Promotes bowel movement, improves blood circulation, forcing spleen and bowel, strengthens immune system, good to fight loss of appetite, flatulence, high blood pressure, depressions, diabetes, constipation, inflammatory bowel disease
Cooking time approx. 25 min
Calories p. portion: 330
6 portions
Allergens: ACGL

Quantity of ingredients:
Wholemeal flour 1/4 lbs - 4oz / 100g. (yes)
Wheat flour 1/4 lbs - 4oz / 100g. (yes)
Chicken egg 4 pieces / 200g. (yes)
Cow's milk (whole milk 3.5% fat) 1 1/2 cups / 400g. (recommended)
Salt 1 pinch / 1g. (yes)
Sunflower oil 1 table spoon / 15g. (recommended)
Olive oil 1 table spoon / 15g. (recommended)
Onion white 1 piece / 50g. (yes)
Parsley 1/2 bunch / 80g. (yes)
Basic recipe for a vegetable soup (nutritious) 1/2 cup / 150g. (yes)
Basil (fresh) 1/4 teaspoon / 1g. (yes)
Nutmeg 1 pinch / 0,3g. (yes)
Créme fraiche cheese 2 table spoons / 45g. (recommended)

Spinach 1,3 lbs / 600g. (yes)
Salt 1 pinch / 1g. (yes)
Pepper (ground) 1 pinch / 0,1g. (yes)
Parmesan 1/8 lbs - 2oz / 60g. (recommended)

Cooking instructions:
Stir flour, eggs and milk and a pinch of salt with the whisk until smooth.
From the dough, fry pancakes crispy brown on both sides.

Heat oil in a small saucepan. Fry the finely chopped onion until tender.
Stir in chopped parsley, sauté briefly. Add the vegetable broth
according to the basic recipe, season with basil and nutmeg. Cover and
simmer for 15 minutes, add crème fraiche and finely puree.
Cook the washed, drizzled spinach with a little salt in a closed pan over
a moderate heat in 3 minutes, drain in a sieve and cut into small pieces.
Add the spinach to the sauce, heat briefly. Add parmesan in the mix.
Fill the pancakes with the cream spinach.

9.32 Plum Cake

Cancer preventive effect, dehydrates the body, stimulates digestion and
binds fats in the intestine, good to fight loss of appetite, flatulence,
inflammatory bowel disease, obesity, gout, stomach ulcers, stomach
cramps, rheumatism, heartburn. Relieves pain, detoxifying, bactericide.
Cooking time approx. 1 hour
Calories p. portion: 502
6 portions
Allergens: AG

Quantity of ingredients:
Curd cheese 20% 5/8 oz / 200g. (yes)
Wheat flour 7/8 lbs / 400g. (yes)
Cow's milk (whole milk 3.5% fat) 6 table spoons / 70g. (recommended)
Rapeseed oil 6 table spoons / 70g. (recommended)
Honey 8 table spoons / 100g. (yes)
Baking powder 1 package / 3g. (yes)
Salt 1 pinch / 1g. (yes)
Cinnamon ground 1 teaspoon / 3g. (yes)
Plums 2,2 lbs / 1000g. (yes)

Cooking instructions:
Mix the flour, curd cheese, milk, oil, honey, salt and baking powder into a smooth dough. Keep the dough cool for 15 minutes to cool.
Lay out baking paper on a baking sheet and press the dough out to a bottom.
Now spread the plums evenly.
Sprinkle the cake with the cinnamon and bake for about 40 minutes at 190 ° C/374 °F.

9.33 Porridge with raisins and sake

Strengthens immune system, improves blood circulation, improves medication effect, stimulates appetite, detoxifies the skin, stimulates nerves, frees breathing, increases body temperature, promotes perspiration.
Cooking time approx. 10 min
Calories p. portion: 427
1 portions
Allergens: AGO

Quantity of ingredients:
Oat flakes (whole grain) 8 table spoons / 60g. (yes)
Water 1/2 cup / 125g. (yes)
Cow's milk (whole milk 3.5% fat) 1/2 cup / 125g. (recommended)
Salt 1 pinch / 1g. (yes)
Cream, sweet 30% 2 table spoons / 20g. (recommended)
Raisins 1 table spoon / 15g. (yes)
Sake 1 table spoon / 10g. (yes)

Cooking instructions:
Heat water and milk and a pinch of salt till it boils. Sprinkle in 4 tablespoons of coarse rolled oats and cook to a pulp, add 4 tablespoons of fine oatmeal, allow to simmer. Arrange in a preheated bowl and top with cream. Add raisins and sake.

9.34 Pumpkin dumplings with tomato and parsley sauce

Protects the digestive system. Good to fight loss of appetite, flatulence, calms nerves and stomach, helps to digest fat, reduces blood pressure, stimulates liver function, dissolves stagnation.
Cooking time approx. 30 min
Calories p. portion: 380

2 portions
Allergens: ACG

Quantity of ingredients:
Hokkaido pumpkin 1/4 lbs - 4oz / 100g. (yes)
Chicken egg 2 pieces / 120g. (yes)
Wheat flour 1/2-1/3 cup / 120g. (yes)
Salt 1 pinch / 1g. (yes)
Pepper (ground) 1 pinch / 0,5g. (yes)
Nutmeg 1 pinch / 0,2g. (yes)
Lemon peel 1/2 teaspoon / 2g. (yes)
Parmesan 2 table spoons / 20g. (recommended)
Onion (spring onion) 2 pieces / 40g. (yes)
Tomato 1/4 lbs - 4oz / 100g. (yes)
Parsley 1/2 bunch / 50g. (yes)
Salt 1 pinch / 1g. (yes)

Cooking instructions:
Peel the pumpkin with a sharp knife, remove the seeds and cut the pulp
into large cubes. Wrap pumpkin in aluminum foil, bake in preheated
oven at 200°C/392°F for 20 minutes. Pour off any spilled pumpkin juice.
Finely crush the pumpkin with the fork. Stir pumpkin and egg until
smooth. Stir in so much flour until a dough is formed, from which
dumplings can be cut off. Season the mixture with lemon zest, salt,
pepper and nutmeg.
Cut off small dumplings with a teaspoon. Leave pumpkin dumplings in
boiling salted water for approx. 7 minutes.

Roast the onion in a frying pan until lightly fry the tomato cubes, salt
and the chopped parsley.

Arrange pumpkin dumplings in portions with the tomato parsley sauce.
Parmesan to hand.

9.35 Raw celery salad

Refreshing, forcing spleen, provides Vitamin C, strengthens digestive
system, detoxifying, improves blood circulation, strengthens liver and
kidney, detoxifying, strengthens the muscles, promotes weight loss.
Cooking time approx. 15 min
Calories p. portion: 590
1 portions
Allergens: HLN

Quantity of ingredients:
Celery root 1/4 piece / 125g. (yes)
Celery sticks 2 branches / 30g. (yes)
Sesame oil 4 table spoons / 40g. (recommended)
Almond puree 2 table spoons / 20g. (yes)
Pepper (ground) 1 pinch / 0,5g. (yes)
Salt 1 pinch / 1g. (yes)
Lemon 1/2 cup / 50g. (yes)
Orange juice 1/2 cup / 60g. (yes)
Peppers powder 1 pinch / 1g. (yes)

Cooking instructions:
Finely grate the celeriac; cut the celeriac into small pieces; celery leaves, cut into small pieces, blanch and combine everything.

Dressing: sesame oil, almond paste, pepper, salt, lemon and fresh orange juice, stir well some rose paprika; mix with the celery and let it pass through.

9.36 Rhubarb cake with sprinkles

Laxative, antipyretic. Protects the digestive system. Detoxifying, affects anorexia, good to fight flatulence, inflammatory bowel disease, brittle nails and hair. Relieves pain, detoxifying, against dry skin, acne, eczema.
Cooking time approx. 1 1/2 hours
Calories p. portion: 476
8 portions
Allergens: AG

Quantity of ingredients:
Wheat flour 7/8 lbs / 400g. (yes)
Cow's milk (whole milk 3.5% fat) 1 cup / 200g. (recommended)
Yeast 1 oz / 30g. (yes)
Honey 2 teaspoons / 5g. (yes)
Sunflower oil 2 teaspoons / 5g. (recommended)
Lemon peel 1 piece / 3g. (yes)
Salt 1 pinch / 1g. (yes)
Rhubarb 2,2 lbs / 800g. (yes)
Margarine 1/4 lbs - 4oz / 120g. (recommended)
Wheat flour 3/4 lbs / 300g. (yes)
Vanilla sugar natural 2 pinches / 1g. (yes)

Cinnamon ground 2 pinches / 1g. (yes)
Honey 5 table spoons / 50g. (yes)

Cooking instructions:
Mix flour, grated lemon peel and salt.
Heat milk gently and mix with yeast and honey.
Then add the flour mixture and the oil and knead vigorously. Cover the dough and let it rise in a warm place until it reaches twice the amount. (about 30 minutes)

For the sprinkles, mix flour with vanilla and cinnamon, then add honey and margarine and crumble to a crumbly mass. Keep the sprinkles dough cool.

Lay out a baking sheet with parchment paper.
Knead the dough for the bottom again, roll it out, place it on the baking sheet and let it rise for another 10 minutes.

Clean the rhubarb, wash it, halve lengthwise and cut into pieces of approx. 3 cm. Spread the pieces on the rolled out dough and crumble the sprinkles over the cake.

Place the cake in the preheated oven at 175 ° C and bake for about 40 minutes.

9.37 Ribbon noodles with leaf spinach

Promotes digestion, improves blood circulation, forcing spleen and intestine, improves pancreatic function, Good to fight loss of appetite, flatulence, inflammatory bowel disease, obesity, stomach ulcers, stomach cramps, rheumatism, heartburn, twelffinger intestinal ulcers.
Cooking time approx. 45 min
Calories p. portion: 722
2 portions
Allergens: ACG

Quantity of ingredients:
Spinach 5/8 lbs - 8oz / 250g. (yes)
Salt 1 pinch / 1g. (yes)
Noodles (wheat, ribbon noodles) with egg 5/8 oz / 200g. (yes)
Olive oil 1 table spoon / 15g. (recommended)
Onion (spring onion) 1 piece / 20g. (yes)
Cream, sweet 30% 1/2 cup / 100g. (recommended)

Créme fraiche cheese 1/2 teaspoon / 6g. (recommended)
Thyme dried 1/2 teaspoon / 2g. (yes)
Basil (fresh) 1/2 teaspoon / 2g. (yes)
Oregano dried 1/2 teaspoon / 2g. (yes)
Nutmeg 1 pinch / 0,5g. (yes)
Pepper (ground) 1 pinch / 0,5g. (yes)
Parmesan 1/2 oz / 20g. (recommended)
Pine nuts 1 table spoon / 15g. (recommended)
Black caraway 1 pinch / 1g. (yes)

Cooking instructions:
Put the dripping wet spinach together with a little salt for 3 minutes in a pot, then drain in a sieve. Then finely cut.

Boil tagliatelle in plenty of salted water.

Heat the oil in a skillet and fry the spring onions rings. Add cream, crème fraiche, thyme, basil, oregano and nutmeg. Stir in the sauce while stirring. Add the spinach, heat briefly, season with nutmeg, salt and pepper.
Drain pasta and mix with the spinach. Season with salt and pepper. Portion noodles and serve with parmesan and pine nuts. Sprinkle the black cumin over it.

9.38 Rice congee with chicken liver and buckthorn fruit

Good to fight blood circulation disorders, thrombose, risk of embolism, high blood pressure, a headache, heart attack and stroke. Has many vitamins and minerals, high quality amino acid profile. Regulates the blood pressure and blood glucose level, forcing spleen.
Cooking time approx. 3 hours
Calories p. portion: 176
3 portions
Allergens: EO

Quantity of ingredients:
Basic recipe for a rice soup (Congee) 5 cups / 800g. (yes)
Chicken liver 1/2 cup / 60g. (yes)
Bocksdorn fruits (Fructus Lycii, Goji, goji berry dried 1/2 cup / 60g. (yes)
Soy sauce 1 dash / 3g. (yes)

Cooking instructions:
Cook basic recipe for rice congee with the chicken liver and wolfberry fruits; Season with soy sauce.

9.39 Rice with parsnips

Rich in vitamins, minerals potassium and zinc. Good to fight blood circulation disorders, thrombose, risk of embolism, high blood pressure, a headache, heart attack and stroke, yeast infections.
Cooking time approx. 45 min
Calories p. portion: 206
3 portions
Allergens:

Quantity of ingredients:
Rice variety any 1 cup / 120g. (yes)
Water 1 1/2 cups / 200g. (yes)
Salt 1 pinch / 1g. (yes)
Parsnip 3-4 pieces / 450g. (yes)
Olive oil 1 table spoon / 10g. (recommended)
Sage 1 teaspoon / 3g. (yes)

Cooking instructions:
Peel the parsnips and cut into slices. Fry for a short time in oil. Add the rice and fry again for a short time. Add the water and cook it at least 30 min. Sprinkle with fresh chopped sage.

9.40 Roasted millet with plum compote

Supports urination, promotes spleen and kidney, strengthens the defense. Good to fight fungi infections.
Cooking time approx. 30 min
Calories p. portion: 139
4 portions
Allergens:

Quantity of ingredients:
Millet 1 cup / 120g. (yes)
Water 1 1/2 cups / 250g. (yes)
Plum 1 1/2 cups / 250g. (yes)
Vanilla pod 1 pinch / 1g. (yes)
Water 5/8 lbs - 8oz / 250g. (yes)
Cinnamon ground 1 pinch / 1g. (yes)
Acerola fruit nectar or powder 1/2 teaspoon / 1g. (yes)

Cooking instructions:
Roast millet briefly, pour over water, heat till it boils and let stand for 20 min. to swell.

Cook plums with water, vanilla and cinnamon 10 min. then strain. Add acerola and add to the millet.

9.41 Salmon on tomato-spinach

Promotes bowel movement, improves blood circulation, forcing spleen and bowel, strengthens blood, reduces inflammation, improves digestion, regenerates skin, supports urination, lowers cholesterol, promotes sweating, dissolves stagnation.
Cooking time approx. 1 hour
Calories p. portion: 365
6 portions
Allergens: D

Quantity of ingredients:
Potato 1,1 lbs / 500g. (yes)
Salt 1 pinch / 1g. (yes)
Salmon 1,3 lbs / 600g. (recommended)
Rapeseed oil 2 teaspoons / 24g. (recommended)
Tomato 1/4 lbs - 4oz / 100g. (yes)
Spinach 1,5 lbs / 700g. (yes)
Salt 1 pinch / 1g. (yes)
Pine nuts 4 table spoons / 40g. (recommended)
Leek 1/4 lbs - 4oz / 120g. (yes)
Olive oil 4 table spoons / 40g. (recommended)
Salt 1 pinch / 1g. (yes)
Pepper white (ground) 1 pinch / 0,5g. (yes)

Cooking instructions:
Peel the potato and cut into cubes, cook in salted water.
Cut the salmon into portions and fry slowly and evenly in a frying pan from both sides, seasoned with salt and pepper, then add the pine nuts and lightly roast.
Blanch spinach in salted water.
Lightly sweat the finely chopped leek with a little rapeseed oil, add the blanched spinach and heat evenly.
Just before serving, add the halved cocktail tomatoes to the spinach and season the vegetables well with salt and pepper.

Arrange the spinach and leek tomato bed with the potatoes, add the salmon and sprinkle with the salted pine nuts.

Drizzle with a little olive oil and serve the dish.

9.42 Scrambled eggs with leaf salad olives and tomatoes

Calms nerves and stomach, relieves fatigue, regulates gastrointestinal function, promotes digestion, stimulates liver function, detoxifying, helps to digest fat, supports urination, reduces blood pressure.
Cooking time approx. 10 min
Calories p. portion: 419
1 portions
Allergens: C

Quantity of ingredients:
Chicken egg 2-3 pieces / 180g. (yes)
Olive oil 1 table spoon / 10g. (recommended)
Salt 1 pinch / 1g. (yes)
Pepper (ground) 1 pinch / 0,5g. (yes)
Olives 6 pieces / 10g. (recommended)
Tomato 1 piece / 50g. (yes)
Lettuce 2 leaves / 5g. (yes)
Turmeric (yellow root) 1 pinch / 1g. (yes)
Parsley 1/2 teaspoon / 5g. (yes)
Basil (fresh) 2-3 leaves / 2g. (yes)

Cooking instructions:
Heat olive oil in the pan. Cut the tomato into a slice. Pluck salad into small pieces. Briefly fry tomatoes, lettuce and olives. Meanwhile mix eggs with salt and spices with a fork.
Pour the egg and spices into the pan. Stir with a wooden spoon until it reaches the desired consistency.
Spices and herbs: turmeric, parsley, basil, black cumin
Variation: zucchini, rocket

9.43 Scrambled eggs with rocket and herbs

Calms nerves and stomach, promotes digestion, detoxifying, strengthens bodily fluids production, promotes perspiration, reduces blood lipids, stimulates, dissolves stagnation, stimulates liver function, harmonizes liver and spleen, strengthens eyesight, detoxifying.
Cooking time approx. 10 min
Calories p. portion: 360
1 portions
Allergens: CG

Quantity of ingredients:
Butter organic 2 table spoons / 20g. (recommended)
Ginger fresh 1 knife tip / 1g. (yes)
Chicken egg 2 pieces / 120g. (yes)
Pepper (ground) 1 pinch / 0,5g. (yes)
Coriander 1 pinch / 1g. (yes)
Parsley 2 table spoons / 16g. (yes)
Rucola 2 handful / 30g. (yes)
Oregano dried 1 teaspoon / 2g. (yes)
Savory 1 pinch / 0,5g. (yes)

Cooking instructions:
Melt a piece of butter in a hot pan; add fine cutted ginger and roast it shortly. Mix in 1 egg whipped, pepper freshly ground, a pinch of coriander, bean cabbage, some salt, parsley chopped, rocket and oregano cut into small pieces until the egg stalls, but still juicy. Garnish: millet, polenta, potatoes, toasted bread. The dish is wholesome, without carbohydrate.

9.44 Sliced chicken with walnuts and sherry

Strengthens blood, strengthens bone marrow, strengthens gastrointestinal function, expands blood vessels, prevents cancer, promotes perspiration, reduces blood lipids, stimulates.
Cooking time approx. 25 min
Calories p. portion: 304
4 portions
Allergens: EGHN

Quantity of ingredients:
Butter organic 2 table spoons / 35g. (recommended)
Walnuts 2 table spoons / 25g. (recommended)
Ginger fresh 1/2 teaspoon / 2g. (yes)

Onion (shallot) 2 pieces / 40g. (yes)
Salt 1 pinch / 1g. (yes)
Chicken meat 3/4 lbs / 300g. (yes)
Peppers powder 1 pinch / 1g. (yes)
Sesame, white 1 teaspoon / 2g. (recommended)
Black fungus mushroom 4 pieces / 3g. (yes)
Shiitake, dried 4 pieces / 5g. (yes)
Soy sauce 1 dash / 3g. (yes)
Rice (whole grain) 1 cup / 120g. (yes)
Water 6 cups / 550g. (yes)
Salt 1 pinch / 1g. (yes)

Cooking instructions:
Heat butter or sesame oil in a hot pan; Sauté walnuts, copious grated ginger, chopped shallots or onions; Add the salt and the sliced chicken and sauté everything; Rose paprika, roasted sesame, soaked black fungus, shiitake mushrooms or mushrooms; with a shot sherry; infuse with water; Simmer for 5 to 10 minutes until the meat is cooked; Season with soy sauce.
Place the rice in salted water, heat till it boils and let it simmer over low heat for about 15 minutes.
This fits: lamb's lettuce, Radicchio

9.45 Spice liqueur

Promotes digestion, nourishes bones and tendons, warms kidneys and spleen, forcing spleen, neutralizes flatulence, controls excessive urge to urinate, helps to fight digestive weakness.
Cooking time approx. 20 min
Calories p. portion: 19
10 portions
Allergens:

Quantity of ingredients:
Chenpi (chinese tangerine bowl) 1/8 lbs - 2oz / 50g. (yes)
Cardamom 1 oz / 30g. (yes)
Sugar candy white 2 table spoons / 20g. (recommended)
Spirit 1 cup / 300g. (yes)

Cooking instructions:
Pour all the ingredients in a wide-mouthed bottle with the schnapps and leave in a dark place for at least 7 days (better still longer).
A glass after a fatty meal regulates stomach energy.

9.46 Spicy avocado cream with cottage cheese

Anti-inflammatory, good to fight swelling, pain and itching, forcing spleen and digestive system, detoxifying, bactericide.
Cooking time approx. 15 min
Calories p. portion: 614
4 portions
Allergens: G

Quantity of ingredients:
Avocado 2 pieces / 600g. (recommended)
Pepper (ground) 1 pinch / 0,5g. (yes)
Salt 1 pinch / 1g. (yes)
Lemon juice 1/2 piece / 15g. (yes)
Peppers powder 1 pinch / 1g. (yes)
Olive oil 1 table spoon / 10g. (recommended)
Herbs various 1 table spoon / 7g. (yes)
Cottage cheese 1 cup / 250g. (yes)
Bread with carob kernel flour 8 slices / 200g. (yes)

Cooking instructions:
Peel, core and purée avocados; add plenty of ground pepper, salt, lemon juice, rose paprika, a few drops of oil, chili, fresh chopped herbs, a pinch of salt; cottage cheese (about the same amount as avocado cream), carefully submerge.

Goes well with: Potatoes and millet, with which the avocado cream in combination with vegetable dishes, legumes or lettuce leaves a delicious meal. It is also very good as an appetizer, as a souvenir at parties and as a morning meal in the summer together with a mild dish of lentils or Adzuki beans and grated radish.

9.47 Spicy cake with dates

Good to fight loss of appetite, flatulence, inflammatory bowel disease, obesity, gout, stomach ulcers, stomach cramps, rheumatism, heartburn. Calms nerves and stomach, improves blood circulation.
Cooking time approx. 1 1/2 hours
Calories p. portion: 808
4 portions
Allergens: ACGO

Quantity of ingredients:
Sunflower oil 1/2 cup / 100g. (recommended)
Sugar white 5/8 oz / 200g. (recommended)
Cow's milk (whole milk 3.5% fat) 1/2 cup / 100g. (recommended)
Wheat flour 5/8 lbs - 8oz / 250g. (yes)
Cocoa 1/8 lbs - 2oz / 40g. (yes)
Dates dried 1/8 lbs - 2oz / 50g. (yes)
Chicken egg 3 pieces / 180g. (yes)
Clove 1/2 teaspoon / 1g. (yes)
Cinnamon ground 1 1/2 tea spoon / 3g. (yes)
Nutmeg 1 pinch / 0,5g. (yes)
Baking powder 1/2 package / 1,5g. (yes)
Butter organic 1 teaspoon / 2g. (recommended)
Wheat flour 1 teaspoon / 2g. (yes)

Cooking instructions:
Separate eggs. Stir egg whites until stiff and set aside.
Add oil, sugar, egg yolk to a bowl and stir until frothy.
Add the flour, cocoa and baking powder, stir. Stir in the milk. Now add the minced dates and the spices (the cloves as grated powder) to the mixture and mix with low speed of the hand mixer.
Now, take the stiffly egg white spoonful carefully under.
Put the dough in a greased, floured mold and bake at 200°C/392°F for 70 minutes.

9.48 Supplementary nutrition

Protein-rich drink with very high energy density. Optimized protein content balances nitrogen losses and promotes protein anabolism.
Cooking time approx. 5 min
Calories p. portion: 1045
1 portions
Allergens:

Quantity of ingredients:
Supplementary nutrition 1 package / 250g. (recommended)

Cooking instructions:
Use only as directed by the physician or therapist.

9.49 Tomato with mozzarella

Promotes digestion, helps to digest fat, supports urination, reduces blood pressure. Affects anorexia, good to fight flatulence, inflammatory bowel disease, bloating and nausea. Relaxing and reassuring.
Cooking time approx. 5 min
Calories p. portion: 436
1 portions
Allergens: AG

Quantity of ingredients:
Mozzarella 1 piece / 50g. (yes)
Tomato 2 pieces / 100g. (yes)
Salt 1 pinch / 1g. (yes)
Basil (fresh) 5 leaves / 6g. (yes)
Olive oil 2 table spoons / 20g. (recommended)
White bread (wheat bread) 2 slices / 40g. (yes)

Cooking instructions:
Cut tomatoes and mozzarella into slices. Serve with salt, basil and olive oil. Serve with white bread.

9.50 Turkey breast with vegetables (Asian)

Strengthens blood, strengthens bone marrow, dissolves stagnation, promotes digestion and is goo to fight high blood pressure. Rice to drain the body at overweight and high blood pressure.
Cooking time approx. 45 min
Calories p. portion: 535
2 portions
Allergens: AEN

Quantity of ingredients:
Rice variety any 1 cup / 120g. (yes)
Water 6 cups / 240g. (yes)
Turkey breast meat 5/8 oz / 200g. (yes)
Ginger fresh 1/3 inch / 3g. (yes)
Garlic 1 piece / 2g. (yes)
Soy sauce 2 table spoons / 20g. (yes)
Wheat flour 2 teaspoons / 15g. (yes)
Onion (spring onion) 2 pieces / 40g. (yes)
Peppers 1/2 piece / 10g. (yes)
Champignon 8 pieces / 30g. (yes)
Sesame oil 2 table spoons / 20g. (recommended)

Soy sauce 1 table spoon / 12g. (yes)
Curry 1 pinch / 2g. (yes)
Turmeric (yellow root) 1 pinch / 2g. (yes)
Cashews 2 teaspoons / 25g. (recommended)

Cooking instructions:
Cook the rice in salted water.
Cut the turkey meat into thin strips. Peel and dice the ginger and garlic.
Put together with the meat strips in a bowl.
Mix 1 tbsp of soy sauce with the wheat starch and stir until smooth. Add
to the meat and marinate for 30 minutes.
Wash spring onions and peppers, clean and cut into small pieces.
Clean and quarter the mushrooms.
Put one tablespoon of sesame oil in a pan and sauté and warm the
marinated turkey. Now add the remaining oil to the pan and fry the other
vegetables in it. Now add the meat and season with soy sauce and
spices. Serve with the rice. Sprinkle the cashews over the dish before
serving.

9.51 Vanilla cream with berries

Weakness, chronic constipation of the intestine, weight loss, laxative,
detoxifying, blood detoxifying. Strengthens the defense. Good to fight
fungi infections.
Cooking time approx. 15 min
Calories p. portion: 278
4 portions
Allergens: G

Quantity of ingredients:
Curd cheese 20% 7/8 lbs / 400g. (yes)
Yogurt (natural, 1.5% fat) 3/8 lbs - 6oz / 150g. (yes)
Sugar brown 2 teaspoons / 8g. (recommended)
Acerola fruit nectar or powder 1 teaspoon / 2g. (yes)
Vanilla sugar natural 3 package / 3g. (yes)
Cream (30% fat) 1/4 lbs - 4oz / 125g. (recommended)
Strawberries 1/4 lbs - 4oz / 100g. (yes)
Raspberry 1/4 lbs - 4oz / 100g. (yes)
Blackberry´s 1/4 lbs - 4oz / 100g. (yes)
Blueberry 1/4 lbs - 4oz / 100g. (yes)

Cooking instructions:
Mix the curd cheese, yoghurt, sugar, acerola and vanilla sugar with a hand mixer or whisk until smooth. Beat the whipped cream very stiff, mix it under the cream. Arrange vanilla cream in portions with the berries.

9.52 Vegetable miso soup with tofu

Very powerful, strengthens after febrile illness, reduces blood pressure, strengthens immune system, prevents cancer, reduces radiation damage, improves blood circulation, strengthens liver and kidney, detoxifying, strengthens the muscles, reduces flatulence, forcing spleen.
Cooking time approx. 15 min
Calories p. portion: 107
4 portions
Allergens: EN

Quantity of ingredients:
Sesame oil 2 table spoons / 35g. (recommended)
Onion (shallot) 1 piece / 20g. (yes)
Carrot 1 piece / 70g. (yes)
Leek 2 inches / 10g. (yes)
Water 3 cups / 750g. (yes)
Endive salad 2 table spoons / 30g. (yes)
Soy Tofu 2 table spoons / 30g. (yes)
Ginger fresh 1/2 teaspoon / 1g. (yes)
Miso 2 table spoons / 15g. (yes)

Cooking instructions:
In sesame oil first sauté onions, then carrots and a little leek; Pour in water and simmer gently; add the bean sprouts and endive leaves and leave to stand; Tofu cubes, add a little ginger; at the end stir in a little cooled cooking-water the Miso.

9.53 Yellow lentil soup

Strengthens heart and kidney, diuretic, promotes spleen, calms the stomach, promotes digestion, strengthens immune system, reduces radiation damage, stimulates liver function, antioxidativ.
Cooking time approx. 20 min
Calories p. portion: 155
7 portions
Allergens: A

Quantity of ingredients:
Lentils yellow 1 lbs / 500g. (yes)
Carrot 2 pieces / 150g. (yes)
Kohlrabi 1 piece / 300g. (yes)
Onion white 1 piece / 50g. (yes)
Parsley 1/2 bunch / 100g. (yes)
Turmeric (yellow root) 1 pinch / 1g. (yes)
Cardamom 1 pinch / 1g. (yes)
Salt 1 pinch / 1g. (yes)
Olive oil 1 table spoon / 10g. (recommended)
Water 4 cup / 1000g. (yes)
Lemon juice 1/2 piece / 15g. (yes)
White bread (wheat bread) 7 slices / 140g. (yes)

Cooking instructions:
Wash lenses well in a colander. Heat oil in a pot. Add finely chopped onion, sliced carrots, diced kohlrabi and spices, sauté and salt. Add the lentils and cover with water and simmer for 20 minutes. Add water as needed and season with salt. Sprinkle with fresh parsley or fresh green cilantro and drizzle with lemon juice.
Here you can also use red lenses. (same cooking time).
Serve with white bread.

9.54 Yogurt with honey and nuts

Relieves pain, detoxifying, promotes wound healing. Good to fight acute or chronic constipation of the intestine. Dissolves stones.
Cooking time approx. 5 min
Calories p. portion: 258
1 portions
Allergens: GH

Quantity of ingredients:
Yogurt (natural, 3.5% fat) 1/4 lbs - 4oz / 125g. (recommended)
Honey 2 table spoons / 30g. (yes)
Walnuts 1 table spoon / 12g. (recommended)

Cooking instructions:
Mix yoghurt with honey and finely chopped nuts.

10 Effects of food

10.1 Use ingredients: recommendable

Acai powder
Almond
Almond marzipan
Anchovy / Sardine
Avocado
Bitter Herb liqueur
Brazil nuts
Brie cheese
Butter organic
Camembert
Cashews
Chestnut puree
Chestnuts
Corn germ oil
Cow's milk (whole milk 3.5% fat)
Cream (30% fat)
Cream 10% coffee cream
Cream sour 30%
Cream, sweet 30%
Créme fraiche cheese
Curd cheese 40%
Duck (slaughtered)
Emmental cheese
Feta cheese
Fox nut, gorgon nut, makhana
Goose
Goose parts
Gorgonzola
Gouda cheese
Hazelnuts
Hibiscus
Kudzu
Lily bulbs
Linseed oil
Mackerel
Maple syrup
Margarine
Margarine (diet)
Mascarpone cheese
Olive oil
Olives
Olives green
Palm oil
Parmesan
Peanut (roasted)
Peanuts
Pine nuts
Pistachios
Poppy
Puff pastry
Pumpkin seed oil
Pumpkin seeds
Rapeseed oil
Salmon
Sesame oil
Sesame oil roasted
Sesame paste (Tahini)
Sesame, black
Sesame, white
Soybean oil
Sugar - icing sugar
Sugar brown
Sugar candy white
Sugar cane sugar
Sugar fructose - fruit sugar
Sugar glucose - grapes sugar
Sugar Milk Sugar
Sugar molasses
Sugar palm sugar
Sugar white
Sunflower oil
Sunflower seeds
Supplementary nutrition
Tuna
Walnut oil
Walnuts
Walnuts roasted
Wheat germ oil
Yogurt (natural, 3.5% fat)

10.2 Use ingredients: yes

Acerola fruit nectar or powder
Adzuki beans
Agar agar (kelp)
Agave nectar
Agrimony
Almond milk
Almond puree
Aloe juice
Amaranth
Amaranth Pops
Angelica root
Anise (Common Fennel)

Apple (sour)
Apple (sweet)
Apple juice (natural cloudy)
Apple puree
Apricot
Apricot dried
Apricot jam
Apricot nectar
Apricots
Apricots juice
Arrowroot
Artichoke
Asparagus (green or white)
Aubergine
Baking powder
Balm
Bamboo shoots
Banana
Banana (cooking banana)
Banchatee (green tea)
barberry
Barley
Barley flour
Barley grass powder
Barley grouts
Barley malt
Barley not peeled
Basic recipe for a beef soup
Basic recipe for a beef soup (warming)
Basic recipe for a chicken soup (warming)
Basic recipe for a duck soup
Basic recipe for a fish soup
Basic recipe for a rice soup (Congee)
Basic recipe for a vegetable soup (nutritious)
Basil
Basil (fresh)
Batavia
Bay leaf
Bean oil
Beans (green, fresh)
Bearberry leaf
Beef bone marrow
Beef fillet
Beef heart
Beef heart (calf)
Beef kidney
Beef liver
Beef lungs (calf)
Beef meat
Beef meat (calf)
Beef meatbones
Beef Oxtail pieces

Beef soup meat
Beef stomach
Beer (alcohol-free)
Beer (alcohol-reduced)
Beer (Pils)
Beer (Top-fermented German dark beer)
Berries of the season
Berry juice
Bitter Lemon
Bitter liqueur
Bitter orange peel
Black beans
Black caraway
Black fungus mushroom
Black tea
Blackberry dried (unripe fruit)
Blackberry jam
Blackberry leaves
Blackberry´s
Black-eyed peas
Blackthorn (Sloe)
Blue mallow tee
Blueberry
Blueberry dried
Blueberry jam
Blueberry juice
Bocksdorn fruits (Fructus Lycii, Goji, goji berry dried
Boletus mushroom
Borage
Borage oil
Boxhorn clover seeds
Bread roll
Bread with carob kernel flour
Breadcrumbs (wheat bread, bread roll)
Broad beans (thick beans)
Broccoli
Brown ale
Brussels sprouts
Buckbean
Buckwheat
Buckwheat (roasted) Kasha
Buckwheat whole grain
Bulgur (cereals)
Burdock root tea
Bush beans
Butter (half fat)
Butter beans white
Buttermilk
Calamari
Campari
Cantaloupe
Capers in olive oil

Carambola (Star fruit)
Cardamom
Carob flour, St. john's bread
Carp
Carrot
Carrot (Early Carrot)
Carrot juice without sugar
Cauliflower
Caviar
Celery root
Celery sticks
Cereal coffee
Chamomile
Chamomile tea
Champignon
Channa-Dal
Chanterelle
Chard
Chenpi (chinese tangerine bowl)
Cherry
Cherry (sour)
Cherry compote
Cherry juice
Chervil
Chervil dried
Chicken Blood
Chicken egg
Chicken egg white
Chicken heart
Chicken liver
Chicken meat
Chicken stomach
Chicken yolk
Chickpeas
Chickweed
Chicory
Chili (pod or ground)
Chinese cabbage
Chinese pearl barley
Chives
Chlorella (fresh water)
Chocolate
Chocolate (Diabetic)
Chrysanthemum blossom tea
Cinnamon ground
Cinnamon sticks
Clarified butter
Clementine
Clementines
Clove
Cocoa
Coconut fat
Coconut flakes
Coconut grated

Coconut meat
Coconut milk
Cod
Codfish
Coffee
Coix (seeds) YiYi Ren
Cola drink
Compote (fruits of the season)
Cooking oil
Coriander
Coriander (fresh)
Corn
Corn (fast polenta)
Corn (roasted)
Corn flour
Corn Grease (Polenta)
Corn silk tea
Corn starch
Cottage cheese
Couscous
Cow's milk (1.5% fat)
Crab
Cranberries
Cranberry
Cranberry
Cranberry jam
Cranberry juice
Cream sour 10%
Cream sour 20%
Creamer
Cress
Crispbread
Crucian
Cucumber
Cucumber (bitter)
Cucumber (spicy cucumber)
Cumin (Caraway seed)
Curcuma
Curd cheese 20%
Currant (black)
Currant (red)
Currant (white)
Currant jam (black)
Currant jam (red)
Currant juice (black)
Currants (black)
Currants (red)
Curry
Curry paste red
Daisy
Dandelion (young plants)
Dandelion juice
Dandelionroots tea
Dashi

Dates dried
Dates red
Deer meat
Deer meat
Deer's Bones
Deer's kidneys
Dill
Duck (heart)
Ducks egg
Dulse (seaweed)
Dyer's broom herb
Edam cheese
Eel
Eel smoked
Elderberries
Elderberry blossom tee
Endive salad
Evening primrose oil
Fennel
Fennel seeds ground
Fennel tea
Fenugreek (Trigonella foenum-
graecum)
Fernet Branca (herbal bitter liqueur)
Feta cheese
Fig
Fig dried
Fish innards
Fish pieces mixed (fresh water)
Fish remains
Fish sauce
Flounder
Flower pollen
French beans
Fresh cheese
Fresh cheese from soya
Fresh cheese with herbs
Freshwater crab
Freshwater fish
Fructose (glucose)
Fruit mix juice
Fruit tea
Gail plum
Galangal
Garam Masala powder
Garlic
Gelatin white
Gelee Royal
Gentian root
Gentian root tea
Ginger fresh
Ginger oil
Ginger powder
Ginkgo fruit

Ginseng
Ginseng liqueur
Ginseng root
Goat
Goat and sheep's blood
Goat and sheep's brain
Goat and sheep's liver
Goat and sheep's milk
Goat and sheep's stomach
Goat cheese
Goose blood
Goose egg
Goose fat
Gooseberry
Gourd
Grape juice red
Grape juice white
Grapefruit (Pomelo)
Grapefruit dried peel
Grapefruit juice
Grapes red
Grapes white
Grapeseed oil
Grass carp
Green spelt
Green tea
Greengage
Ground
Ground caraway
Guava
Halibut (Flatfish)
Hawthorn
Herbal tea mix
Herbs bitter
Herbs of Provence
Herbs various
Herbs wild
Herring
Hibiscus tea
Hijiki
Hokkaido pumpkin
Honey
Honey wine (Met)
Hop
Horehound leaves
Horse meat
Hyssop
Iceberg lettuce
Jasmine blossoms tee
Jellyfish
Juniper berry
Kaki plum
Kalmus
Kefir

Kidney beans (red)
King Solomon's-seal
Kiwi
Kohlrabi
Kombu seaweed (Saccharina japonica)
Kukicha tea
Kumquats
Ladyfingers
Lamb bones
Lamb kidneys
Lamb liver
Lamb meat
Lamb shoulder
Lamb's lettuce
Lamb's lettuce
Lavender blossoms
Leaf salads (bitter)
Leek
Lemon
Lemon Balm (dried)
Lemon Balm (fresh)
Lemon juice
Lemon peel
Lemongrass
Lentils
Lentils black
Lentils red
Lentils yellow
Lettuce
Licorice root tea
Lima beans
Lime
Lime blossom tea
Linseed
Linseed (crushed)
Liver smoothing tea
Lobster
Longane
Loquate / Japanese medlar
Lotus roots
Lotus seeds
Lovage
Lovage seeds
Luo Han Guo fruit
Lychee
Lychee in Preserved
Lychee liqueur
Lye roll
Mallow (Malva sylvestris) blossom tea
Malt
Mango
Mango juice
Manioc flour
Mare's milk

Marjoram
Martini
Mayonnaise 50%
Mayonnaise 80%
Mediterranean fish (cod, plaice, haddock, sea eel, mackerel)
Medlar
Millet
Millet flakes
Mineral water
Mirabelle plum
Miso
Miso black (fermented)
Miso paste (soy bean paste)
Mixed Pickles
Mold cheese
Morel (black, dried)
Morel, dried
Mozzarella
Mu Erh Mushroom
Muesli
Mulberry fruit
Mulled Wine Spice
Mullet
Multi-grain bread (gray bread)
Mung bean
Mung bean sprouting
Mussels
Mustard
Mustard Dijon
Mustard medium hot
Mustard seeds
Mustard sweet
Mutton
Mutton
Nasturtium (nose-twister or nose-tweaker)
Nectarine
Nettles
Noodles (wheat) with egg
Noodles (wheat, lasagne) with egg
Noodles (wheat, ribbon noodles) with egg
Noodles (wheat, spaghetti) with egg
Noodles (whole grain) with egg
Nori, purple seaweed, red algae
Nutmeg
Oat
Oat flakes (whole grain)
Oat flakes roasted
Oat flour
Oat fusion (baby food)
Oat meal
Oat milk

Octopus
Octopus
Okra
Onion (shallot)
Onion (spring onion)
Onion read
Onion white
Orange
Orange blossom
Orange dried peel
Orange grated peel
Orange jam
Orange juice
Orange peel
Oregano dried
Oregano fresh
Oyster mushroom
Oyster shell powder
Oysters
Papaya
Parsley
Parsley root
Parsnip
Passion blossoms tea
Passion fruit
Peaches
Peaches (canned)
Peanut butter
Peanut oil
Pear
Pear juice
Pearl barley
Pearl barley
Peas
Peas, green
Pepper (ground)
Pepper Cayenne
Pepper powder (hot)
Pepper white (ground)
Peppercorns
Peppermint
Peppermint tea
Pepperoni
Pepperoni, red, pitted, halved
Pepperoni, yellow, pitted, halved
Peppers
Peppers (rose peppers)
Peppers (sweet)
Peppers powder
Perch
Pheasant
Pickle
Pig blood
Pigeon

Pigeon egg
Pimento
Pineapple
Pineapple (from a can)
Pineapple juice without sugar
Pinto beans speckled
Plaice
Plum
Plum dried
Plums
Pomegranate
Pork Bacon
Pork brain
Pork fat (lard)
Pork ham
Pork ham cooked
Pork ham smoked
Pork heart
Pork kidneys
Pork knuckle
Pork Lard
Pork liver
Pork lung
Pork marrow bones
Pork meat
Pork sausage (Bratwurst)
Pork skin
Pork stomach
Pork/beef sausage (smoked)
Pork's intestine
Potato
Potato (mealy)
Potato flour
Prickly pear
Processed cheese 12%
processed cheese 30%
Prosecco
Psyllium seed
Pudding powder vanilla
Pumpernickel (dark bread)
Pumpkin
Quail
Quail egg
Quince
Quinoa
Rabbit
Rabbit (wild)
Rabbit liver
Rabbit meat
Radicchio
Radish
Radish (white, green, purple-red)
Radish black
Radish horseradish

Radish leaves
Raisins
Raspberry
Raspberry dried (immature)
Raspberry jam
Raspberry leaf tea
Red beet
Red berry (without sugar)
Red cabbage
Red wine
Reishi mushroom
Rhubarb
Ribworttea
Rice (fragrance)
Rice (Gaoliang / Sorghum)
Rice (whole grain)
Rice Basmati
Rice black
Rice flour
Rice long grain rice
Rice malt
Rice mash
Rice noodles
Rice red
Rice round grain
Rice starch
Rice sticky
Rice sweet
Rice variety any
Rice wild (nature rice)
Romaine lettuce / lettuce salad
Rose blossom tea
Rose hip
Rose hip tea
Rose leaf tea
Rosefish
Rosemary
Rucola
Rum
Rusk
Rye
Rye flour
Rye wholemeal bread
Safflower (Dyer's thistle / Hong Hua)
Saffron
Sage
Sago (cereals)
Sake
Salsify
Salt
Salt (herbal)
Sauerkraut (cutted cabbage fermented)
Savory
Savoy cabbage / kale

Sea buckthorn
Sea cucumber
Seacrab
Shark
Sheep's milk
Sheep's milk yoghurt
Sherry (whine)
Shiitake, dried
Shrimp
Shrimps
Skim milk powder
Slug
Sorrel
Sour cherries
Sour cream 15% fat
Sour milk
Sour milk cheese 20%
Sourdough
Soy flour
Soy noodles
Soy sauce
Soy Tofu
Soy Tofu smoked
Soya Cuisine (soy cream)
Soybean milk
Soybeans
Soybeans, black
Soybeans, blacks, fermented
Soybeans, yellow
Spelled (Dark) bread
Spelled flakes
Spelled grain
Spelled semolina
Spelled wholemeal flour
Spinach
Spiny lobsters
Spirit
Spurdog (spiny dogfish, Schillerlocken)
St. Benedict's thistle, blessed thistle,
holy thistle, spotted thistle
Star anise
Strawberries
Strawberry jam
Strawberry Juice
Sweet potato
Tabasco
Tangerine
Tarragon (Estragon)
Tea mixture uric acid lowering
Thistle oil
Thyme
Thyme dried
Toast bread (whole grain)
Tomato

Tomato dried
Tomato juice
Tomato paste
Tomato puree
Tonic Water
Topinambur
Trout
Trout (smoked)
Truffle
Tsampa (roasted barley flour)
Turkey breast meat
Turkey ham
Turmeric (yellow root)
Turnip
Turnips
Umeboshi paste
Umeboshi plums (Japanese apricots)
Valerian
Vanilla
Vanilla pod
Vanilla powder
Vanilla sugar natural
Vegetable juice
Vinegar (Apple vinegar)
Vinegar (Red wine vinegar)
Vinegar Aceto Balsamico
Vinegar Aceto Balsamico white
Wakame
Water
Water hot
Watermelon
Wax gourd
Wheat
Wheat beer
Wheat bran
Wheat bulgur
Wheat flakes

Wheat flatbread/pita bread
Wheat flour
Wheat flour whole grain
Wheat semolina
Wheat semolina for children
Wheat/Rye/Gray-black bread with yeast
Wheatgrass juice
Wheatgrass powder
Whey
White beans
White bread (baguette)
White bread (pretzel sticks)
White bread (roll)
White bread (wheat bread)
White breadcrumbs
White cabbage
White dumpling bread (wheat bread cut into chunks)
White wine
Whitefish
Whole grain bread
Wholemeal flour
Wild boar meat
Wild garlic (garlic spinach)
Wild herbs
Wild strawberries
Wormwood
Wormwood herb
Yam root, yam root tuber
Yarrow
Yarrow tea
Yeast
Yew nut
Yoghurt vanilla
Yogi tea
Yogurt (natural, 1.5% fat)
Zucchini

10.3 Use ingredients: little

-

10.4 Do not use contra-acting foods

Cola drink (low calorie)
Stevia (candyleaf, sweetleaf)

Sugar substitute (sweetener)

11 Herbs and their effects

11.1 Basil (fresh)

It has a beneficial effect on flatulence and nausea, relaxing and soothing. Good to fight emphysema, bronchitis, whooping cough, high blood pressure, headache, mouth odor, warts, hiccup, gout, migraine.

11.2 Mugwort

Reduces bleeding, alleviates pain. In the kitchen, mugwort is used as a spice for fat food. Since it contains many bitter substances, it boosts fat burning and promotes digestion.

11.3 Savory

Stomach-strengthening, soothing and appetizing. Ideal for prevent colds, strengthens the immune system. In case of incontinence or nocturnal wetting (not for children), put the beans in liquor for libido.

11.4 Coriander

The essential oils are appetizing, digestive, cramping and soothing in stomach and intestinal disorders.

11.5 Herbs various

Appetizing, lots of trace elements and vitamins

11.6 Lovage

Stimulates digestion, reduces pain. Extracts of the root are used to flush out urinary tract infections and prevent kidney gravel.

11.7 Oregano dried

It has an anti-digestive, calming and nerve-strengthening effect, helps to fight cramping stomach and intestinal disorders. The ingredient Carvacrol has an anti-inflammatory effect.

11.8 Parsley

Stimulates liver function, detoxifies. Forces urinating. Relieves flatulence. Digestive and menstrual stimulating, birth-accelerating, memory-enhancing, blood-purifying, skin-smoothing.

11.9 Sage

Good to fight yeast infections. The leaves have a digestive effect and are used in greasy foods. Antiperspirant effect. Helps to relieve coughing attacks. Dries out (TCM).

11.10   Black caraway

Detoxifying, immunoregulatory. In addition, the oil should stimulate the formation of bone marrow cells and generally protect body cells from viruses.

11.11   Thyme dried

Disinfecting. It stimulates the blood circulation, increases the appetite and helps to digest fat meat better. Strengthens lungs and spleen (TCM).

11.12   Lemon Balm (fresh)

Stimulating, antibacterial, encouraging, relaxing, antispasmodic, cooling, antipyretic, analgesic, sweat-inducing, virus-inhibiting. Good for colds, fever, flu, cough, bronchitis, asthma, loss of appetite, bloating, heartburn.

12 Basics of Nutrition

The basic principles of nutrition described herein are general recommendations. They are not aimed at a specific form of therapy. Recommendations concerning a therapy have priority.

12.1 Nutrition

Regular meals in a relaxed atmosphere. A warm breakfast is considered a good start into the day.
The main meals ought to be taken for lunch – supper in the early evening. Pay attention to feeling hungry or sated: don't eat too much nor remain hungry is the rule
Prepare the meals freshly from natural, regional products. Frozen, heat-conserved, industrially prepared or foodstuffs cooked in the microwave oven are rejected.
Choice of foodstuffs according to the season: more cooling food in summer, more warming food in winter.
Eat cooked food at least twice a day. Food and drinks ought to be lukewarm, never ice-cold or hot.
Raw vegetables, briefly cooked vegetables, freshly squeezed juices and mineral water are not recommended. Milk and dairy products are only included in the diet if they don't cause problems.
Don't use therapeutic recipes over a longer period without consulting your doctor or therapist.

Varied food
Enjoy the diversity of foodstuffs. Characteristics of a balanced nutrition are variety, suitable combination and a balanced quantity of rich and low energy foodstuffs (on one hand avoiding undersupply with essential nutrients and on the other hand to take to many undesirable substances).

A lot of Cereal Products - and Potatoes
Bread, pasta, rice, cereal flakes (best wholemeal) as well as potatoes contain almost no fat, but many vitamins, mineral nutrients, trace elements, roughage and secondary plant substances. These foodstuffs ought to be taken with low-fat side dishes.

Vegetables and Fruit – „Take Five" every day ...
5 portions of vegetables and fruit a day, as fresh as possible, briefly cooked, or maybe one portion as a juice – ideal as a side dish to every meal as well as snack between meals: Thus a lot of vitamins, mineral nutrients as well as roughage and secondary plant substances

Daily milk and dairy products
Milk and Dairy Products every Day, once or twice per Week Fish; meat, sausages as well as eggs moderately. These foodstuffs contain valuable nutrients like calcium in the milk, iodine selenium and omega-3 fat acids in saltwater fish. Meat is favorable due to its high content of disposable iron and the vitamins B1, B6 and B12. Quantities of 300 – 600 g meat and sausage per week are sufficient. Prefer low-fat products, especially in meat- and dairy products.

Low-fat and fatty Foodstuffs
Fat supplies us with essential fat acids and fatty foodstuffs contain also fat-soluble vitamins. Fat is high in energy; therefore much fat in the food may cause overweight, possibly also cancer. Too many saturated fat acids may further a tendency for cardio-vascular diseases in the long term. Prefer vegetable oils and fats (e.g. rapeseed-, olive-, soya-oils and solid fats produced therefrom). Beware of invisible fat in meat- and dairy products, pastry and sweets as well as in fast-food and convenience foods. 70 – 90 g fat per day is sufficient.

Moderately Sugar and Salt
Take sugar and foods/drinks containing various kinds of sugar (e.g. glucose syrup) only occasionally. Use herbs and spices as well as a little salt creatively. Prefer salt containing iodine.

Plenty of Liquids
Water is absolutely essential. Drink 1-2 l liquids every day. Prefer water (with or without gas) and other low-calorie drinks. Alcoholic drinks should not be taken.

Tasty Dishes, carefully cooked
Cook the meals with as low temperatures and as short as possible, using little water and fat – this preserves the original taste, keeps the nutrients intact and prevents the production of harmful compounds.

Take time and enjoy the food
Take your Time and enjoy your Food
Eating consciously helps to eat right. The eye enjoys food, too. It's fun, invites to enjoy varied dishes and stimulates the feeling of satiety.

Watch your Weight and stay in Motion
A balanced diet and a lot of exercise and sport (30 – 60 min/day) are a healthy combination. The right weight furthers well-being and health. Thermals, directional effectiveness, digestive power

There are various criteria for judging the effectiveness of herbs and foodstuffs.

The use of certain herbs and ingredients is based on observations of the effects on the body which these foodstuffs, herbs and spices show after having eaten them. The medical science has developed following system: Every ingredient or herb has a directional effectiveness. Furthermore, there are herbs which have a special effect on certain organs.

The basic condition for a healthy metabolism is to obtain sufficient energy from food and that the digestive process doesn't use too much energy. An easily digestible meal makes content and sated, doesn't cause flatulence and fatigue after the meal. The perfect spices increase the healthiness of our meals. Very often, just small doses of herbs and spices will suffice. They are not used to make us sated, but to help our digestive organs to digest the food.

12.2 Recipes

The recipes list the ingredients to be used and the cooking instructions show how the dish is prepared. The list of ingredients shows the concerned quantities as well as the relevance for the therapy. If you find „less than mentioned", try to comply or find an alternative from the „list of recommended foodstuffs". Mostly it shall result just in a small change of taste when you simply avoid this ingredient.

Mild cooking methods: boiling, stewing, poaching, steaming
Strong cooking methods: barbecuing, roasting, frying, smoking
Balanced cooking methods: deep-frying, baking brick
Deep-freezing and warming in the microwave oven should be avoided (denaturalization).

12.3 Foodstuffs

Foodstuffs have an effect on body and soul like medicinal herbs, only a very much milder one. Dietary advice is mainly based on regional foodstuffs. The knowledge about the effects of each foodstuff and the knowledge, when which foodstuff shall be used, is based on the orthodoschool of medicine. Use ecologic-organic products, if possible. As everything should be cooked for a long time due to a better digestability and very rarely eaten raw, the food agrees with everyone.

The classification of the foodstuffs according to their effect on the body is the basis in order to achieve a harmonious status of health.

Dietary advisors do not recommend certain foodstuffs for everyone. The individual diet is tailor-made for the individual constitution.

Buy only fresh and ripe fruit and vegetables. You ought to leave unripe fruit and vegetables and such with brown spots and wilted leaves behind in the market. In this case take deep-frozen goods (never ready-to-serve dishes!). Fruit and vegetables are deep-frozen immediately after harvesting and often contain more vitamins and minerals than the goods from the vegetable shelf. Whereas conserved or tinned goods contain very much less biological substances. Also, salt, sugar and others are mostly added to the latter. Never leave the foodstuffs in the water after washing them to avoid that many vital substances get drowned. Clean salads, fruit and vegetables immediately before serving.

Please make sure of the hygienic processing of foodstuffs. Clean your salads, fruit and vegetables carefully. When cooking with meat, prepare all ingredients first and then process the meat products. Clean the worktop and tools very carefully. Wooden surfaces ought to be treated with a mild disinfectant regularly in order to reduce germination.

Store fruit and vegetables separately, if possible. Harvested fruit and vegetables are still alive and emit e.g. ethylene gas, which makes other products ripen and age faster. Keep meat and fish in the closed packaging or store them in the fridge in closed containers.

12.4 Herbs

There are some basic rules for storing medicinal herbs. On principle, herbs must be protected from direct sunlight, humidity and heat.

Containers for the storage of herbs may be glasses, ceramic jars and even plastic containers. However, plastic is a rather unsuitable material and should only be a short-term solution. In case of glass containers, use a dark material.

Medicinal herbs cannot be kept for any long period. The shelf life of herbs is limited. However, it can be prolonged with suitable storage. The place should be dark, rather cool and absolutely dry. A wooden medicine cabinet, placed not directly next to a source of heat, would be ideal. Never buy large quantities of herbs so as not to have to throw them away. Label the container with the name of the herb and the date of harvesting or processing.

13 Other dietic-books

The following syndromes of dietetics, TCM or for a therapy supplement for cancer are available.

Dietetics

E001. Nutrition of the infant - baby food
E002. Nutrition during lactation
E003. Nutrition in old age
E004. Nutrition of children and adolescents
E005. Nutrition of athletes
E006. Light weight
E007. Pregnancy
E008. Full food

Protein and electrolyte - kidneys
E009. (hemodialysis) dialysis treatment
E010. Acute renal failure
E011. Chronic renal insufficiency
E012. Nephrotic syndrome
E013. Kidney stones (nephrolithiasis)

Gastrointestinal tract - pancreas
E014. Acute pancreatitis (inflammation of the pancreas)
E015. Chronic pancreatitis (inflammation of the pancreas)

Gastrointestinal tract - small intestine and large intestine
E016. Acute obstipation (constipation)
E017. Chronic obstipation (constipation)
E018. Colon irritabile
E019. Diverticulitis
E020. Acquired lactose intolerance (lactose malabsorption)
E021. Fructose malabsorption
E022. Glutensensitive enteropathy (celiac disease)
E023. Colectomy
E024. Short Bowel Syndrome

Gastrointestinal tract - liver, gallbladder, bile ducts
E025. Acute and chronic hepatitis (inflammation of the liver)
E026. Cholelithiasis (bile stones)
E027. fatty liver
E028. cirrhosis

Gastrointestinal tract - Stomach and duodenal intestine
E029. Acute gastritis
E030. Chronic gastritis
E031. Stomach bleeding
E032. Ulcus ventriculi and duodenal ulcer
E033. Condition after gastric surgery

Gastrointestinal tract - oral cavity and esophagus
E034. Stomatitis
E035. Esophageal carcinoma (esophageal cancer)
E036. Refluosophagitis (heartburn)

Special diseases
E037. Phenylketonuria (PKU)
E038. Rheumatic joint diseases

Metabolism
E039. Obesity (overweight)
E040. Diabetes mellitus
E041. Eating disorders (underweight)

Fat metabolism
E042. Hypercholesterolaemia (increased cholesterol level)
E043. Hepatic Encephalopathy

Heart and circulation
E044. Arteriosclerosis (arterial calcification)
E045. Heart insufficiency
E046. Hypertension
E047. Hyperuricaemia and gout

Changed nutrient requirements
E048. In case of fever
E049. For malignant diseases
E050. After burns
E051. Radiation and chemotherapy

CANCER
E100. Pancreatic cancer
E101. Bladder cancer
E102. Blood cancer (leukemia)
E103. Breast cancer
E104. Colorectal cancer
E105. Gastric cancer
E106. Kidney cancer
E107. Esophageal cancer

TCM
E200. Bladder - moisture heat in the bladder
E201. Bladder - moisture and cold in the bladder
E202. Bladder - emptiness and cold in the bladder
E203. Large intestine - external cold affects the large intestine
E204. Large intestine - moisture heat in the large intestine
E205. Large intestine - heat blocks the intestine II acute
E206. Large intestine - dryness of the colon
E207. Large intestine - Yang deficiency (cold)
E208. Heart - Blood insufficiency
E209. Heart - Blood stagnation
E210. Heart - Fire
E211. Heart - Hot mucus clogs the heart pores

E212. Heart - Cold mucus clogs the heart pores
E213. Heart - Qi deficiency
E214. Heart - Yang deficiency
E215. Heart - Yin deficiency
E216. Liver - Ascending Liver Yang
E217. Liver - Blood deficiency
E218. Liver - Blood stagnation
E219. Liver - Moisture heat in liver and gall bladder
E220. Liver - Fire
E221. Liver - Gall bladder Qi-Empty
E222. Liver - Cold in the liver meridian
E223. Liver - Qi stagnation
E224. Liver - Wind
E225. Liver - Wind with ascending liver Yang
E226. Liver - Wind with blood anemic
E227. Liver - Wind with extreme heat
E228. Lung - Qi deficiency
E229. Lung - Mucus-moisture in the lungs
E230. Lung - Mucus-heat in the lungs
E231. Lung - Mucus-cold in the lungs
E232. Lung - Dryness of the lungs
E233. Lung - Wind-heat attacks the lungs
E234. Lung - Wind-cold affects the lungs
E235. Lung - Yin deficiency
E236. Stomach - Bloodstagnation
E237. Stomach - Fire
E238. Stomach - Cold with liquid
E239. Stomach - Nutrition stagnation
E240. Stomach - Qi deficiency
E241. Stomach - Rebellious Qi
E242. Stomach - Yin Emptiness
E243. Spleen - Heat and moisture attack the spleen
E244. Spleen - Coldness and moisture affects the spleen
E245. Spleen - Qi deficiency
E246. Spleen - Qi deficiency + Declining spleen Qi
E247. Spleen - Qi deficiency + spleen does not control the blood
E248. Spleen - Yang deficiency
E249. Kidney - Heart and kidney no longer communicate
E250. Kidney - Jing deficiency
E251. Kidney - Kidneys cannot receive the Qi
E252. Kidney - Qi is not stable
E253. Kidney - Yang deficiency
E254. Kidney - Yin deficiency

For further information visit di-book.com.